NO EASY CHOICE

Written under the auspices of the
Center for International Affairs,
Harvard University

NO EASY CHOICE

Political Participation
in Developing Countries

Samuel P. Huntington

Joan M. Nelson

HARVARD UNIVERSITY PRESS
Cambridge, Massachusetts, and London, England

Second printing 1977

Library of Congress Cataloging in Publication Data

Huntington, Samuel P
  No easy choice.

  "This study grows out of a research program conducted from 1969 to 1973 at
the Center for International Affairs of Harvard University."
  Bibliography: p.
  Includes index.
  1. Underdeveloped areas—Political participation. I. Nelson, Joan M., joint
author. II. Harvard University. Center for International Affairs. III. Title.
JF60.H85   320.9'172'4   75-31883
ISBN 0-674-62530-7

Preface

This study grows out of a research program conducted from 1969 to 1973 at the Center for International Affairs of Harvard University. The program focused on the determinants and patterns of political participation in developing nations and on the interaction between political participation and certain aspects of economic and social modernization. Eleven scholars contributed to the program, using a variety of methodologies and approaches. Included in the program were case studies of four countries, exploring patterns of political participation in Colombia, Kenya, Pakistan, and Turkey. Also part of the program were cross-national studies of participation patterns among two low-income groups: the peasantry and the urban poor. These were supplemented by intensive analyses of participation by these groups in particular nations: the urban poor in Mexico and villagers in Vietnam. Finally, the program included support for the development of two theoretical and quantitative models of participation.

This multi-faceted approach reflected our belief that many other studies of political participation had suffered from too exclusive a reliance on one methodology or another. Studies and models using aggregate data at the national level must confront the fact that national totals, percentages, or averages often conceal such vast variations within nations as to be almost meaningless. Moreover, cross-national comparisons tend to minimize attention to dynamic and developmental factors. The survey approach, on the other hand, often becomes divorced from its social and institutional contexts: explanations for patterns of participation are sought largely as a function of individual attitudes and status characteristics. Case studies have obvious advantages in depth and appreciation of dynamic sequences; they provide rich material for more general theories and explanations, even though they cannot offer any themselves. By combining country studies, comparative sector studies, and aggregate modeling, we hoped to draw on the insights of each while not being restricted by their weaknesses.

The present essay was originally a substantive report to the Agency for International Development, which provided the bulk of the funding for the research program. The report was both more and less than a summary of that program. While we could not attempt to summarize all the findings from each of the individual studies in the program, we did seek to integrate some of the key contributions of these studies into a broader perspective on political participation. We also attempted to marry the research done by members of the Harvard group with the closely related work of other scholars dealing with political participation. As our footnotes make clear, however, we have drawn most heavily on the studies produced by the Harvard project. Our study is not a comprehensive analysis of political participation nor even of the relations between social and economic change and political participation in developing countries. It focuses, instead, on those aspects of these topics that were dealt with in the Harvard program. It is thus in part a research report, in part an effort at summary and generalization from recent studies of political participation, and in part a theoretical essay suggesting an approach and concepts that can be used to analyse political participation. We have been particularly concerned with the processes through which previously non-participant groups and individuals are incorporated into the political arena. Our emphasis is on political participation as the dependent variable, rather than as a causal factor influencing other trends.

This volume is the joint product of the happy, if temporary, convergence of the scholarly interests of its two authors. In *Political Order in Changing Societies* (Yale University Press, 1968), Huntington argued that political stability rested in large part on the relation between political institutionalization and political participation. Socio-economic modernization promoted the decay of political institutions and the expansion of political participation, which, in turn, led to political instability and violence. The current volume takes off from this analysis, with attention now focused on political participation rather than political stability as the central dependent variable. The expansion of political participation is found to be more the by-product of socio-economic modernization than the conscious first-choice of individuals, groups, or elites. In a subsequent volume, Huntington plans to carry forward the analyses of these two books and to elaborate the relationships (briefly presented in Chapter 2 of this book) among political stability, political participation, economic wealth, socio-economic equity, and national autonomy. Nelson's interest in political participation grows out of her earlier critique of theories linking political instability, cityward migration, and the urban poor. Better theories about the political role of the poor demand broader and more flexible concepts of political participation itself, and a fuller recognition of the various channels through which the poor may become participant. This study develops such concepts; a forthcoming study develops them in more detail with specific reference to the urban poor.

Our intellectual debt is particularly great to our colleagues in the original research program: Henry Bienen, Michael Brower, Ronald Brunner, Shahid Burki, Wayne Cornelius, Ergun Özbudun, Samuel L. Popkin, John D. Powell, and William Schneider. We are grateful to the Agency for International Development for the research grant that supported the program. Certain portions of Chapter 3 have appeared in briefer and different form in Samuel P. Huntington and Jorge I. Domínguez, "Political Development," in Fred Greenstein and Nelson Polsby, eds., *Handbook of Political Science* (Reading, Mass.: Addison-Wesley, 1975), Vol. III, pp. 33-47, and are adapted for use here with the permission of Addison-Wesley. We would also like to thank Gabriel Almond, Alex Inkeles, Princeton Lyman, John D. Powell, Lucian Pye, and Sidney Verba for helpful comments on earlier drafts of this study. Anna Larson and Barbara Talhouni efficiently typed what seemed like unending manuscript drafts. Needless to say, while our debts are many, responsibility for facts and judgments in this study lies with us alone.

S.P.H.
J.M.N.

Contents

Contents

NO EASY CHOICE

Introduction:
The Nature
of Political
Participation

The Role of Participation

Broadening political participation is a hallmark of political modernization. In traditional society, government and politics are usually the concern of a narrow elite. The peasants, artisans, and traders who make up the bulk of the population may or may not recognize how the government's actions affect their own lives. But it would not normally occur to them that it was feasible or desirable to try to influence governmental actions, save for a rare petition for relief from outside stress. In contrast, the principle of active citizenship is accepted and emphasized in all modern industrial states, although the forms and nature of legitimate participation vary widely.

This study focuses on the processes through which participation broadens, including the aggregate social, economic, and political forces that bear on participation, and also the more specific channels of participation that are likely to activate individuals and groups who were formerly nonparticipant. In the long run, social and economic modernization produces broadened participation. But the processes are neither steady, uniform, nor irreversible. Some nations have far higher levels of participation than their stage of socio-economic development would seem to warrant; others have far less. The same is true for groups within nations. Moreover, participation rates in groups or nations may drop precipitously and forms of participation can change dramatically. The relationships between growth or modernization and political participation are complex and are mediated by a number of additional factors.

Political participation in developing countries has taken on a relevance that goes considerably beyond the interests of academic political

1

scientists. The past decade has seen increasing disenchantment with accelerated economic growth as the major means of increasing welfare and equity in the developing nations. This disenchantment was clearly stated by World Bank President Robert S. McNamara in his address in September 1972 to the Board of Governors of the World Bank Group:[1]

> It is becoming increasingly clear that the critical issue within developing countries is not simply the pace of growth, but the nature of growth. The developing nations achieved an overall average annual GNP growth rate of more than the targeted 5% by the end of the sixties. But the social impact of that growth was so severely skewed, and the numbers of individuals all but passed by so absolutely immense, that the simple statistical achievement of that target was misleading.

In short, an increased GNP does not automatically lead to more equitable income distribution, fuller access for less privileged groups to education and productive employment, a balanced and healthy long-run pattern of urban development, or other goals of modernization.

In most developing nations more equitable growth demands a reorientation of social and economic policies and programs. This reorientation is primarily the task of the developing nations themselves. It is, in the first instance, a political problem. In McNamara's words, "The developing countries must decide for themselves if they wish to undertake it. It will manifestly require immense resolve and courage."[2] The difficulty, of course, is that those who benefit from the status quo, or hope to do so, will usually resist reform, and they are also usually powerful.

Reform will be opposed not only by a narrow wealthy elite, but also by a much broader range of middle- and upper-middle-class people. These people are not wealthy by the standards of the industrialized nations; they are usually aware of this and would resent being described as a privileged elite. Yet, by comparison with most of their compatriots, they are privileged. While they support and often demand a variety of reforms, they are not prepared to go along with changes that would sacrifice their own aspirations, much less their current standard of living. Although the middle and upper-middle classes are a smaller part of the total population in developing nations than in industrialized nations, their numbers are often substantial and their voice in politics still more so.

Political leaders, in power or aspiring to power, must overcome elite and middle-class resistance if they wish to reorient development policies. They can choose among, or combine, three basic strategies to this end. Some segments of the upper and middle classes can be persuaded to drop or soften their opposition. Leaders (most of whom themselves are from elite or middle-class backgrounds) can appeal to ideological principles, nationalist fervor, or long-run enlightened self-interest. Sometimes they can bargain for support, offering compensation to individuals or groups for their concessions. The second possible strategy is simple repression. This obviously demands a loyal and efficient military and police force. The third strategy is political mobilization of groups that were previously passive, or active but ineffective, in order to counterbalance or override opposition. In other words, the reformer may seek support in broadened political participation.

By political participation we mean activity by private citizens designed to influence government decision-making. Participation may be individual or collective, organized or spontaneous, sustained or sporadic, peaceful or violent, legal or illegal, effective or ineffective.[3] Effective support for a substantial shift in economic or social policies is most likely to come from organized collective participation, which can assume a variety of forms.

Neither persuasion nor pure repression is normally effective for more than limited groups or limited issues. Effective reform almost always requires changes in political participation, usually in combination with some degree of persuasion or repression. This holds in most political systems, including traditional monarchies attempting to introduce moderate reform, competitive parliamentary systems, and single-party development-oriented states. Economic and social reform in nineteenth-century England was accompanied and largely generated by periodic expansion of the electorate. A modernizing monarch appeals to middle-class groups against conservative elites, and to loyal and traditional peasants against impatient (and sometimes self-seeking) middle-class groups. A socialist revolution, whether by force or through more peaceful means (as in Chile between 1970 and 1973), mobilizes urban workers and peasants on a massive scale to counterbalance and overcome resistance from the middle and upper classes. A fuller understanding of the determinants and patterns of political participation can benefit not only those who simply seek to understand trends and events in developing nations, but also those who would like to intervene in favor of greater equity.

A Core Definition of Political Participation

The term "political participation" has been used to mean various things. Is political participation behavior only, or does it also encompass the attitudes and perceptions prerequisite to participatory behavior (for example: political information, perception of the relevance of politics to one's own concerns, a belief that one can influence governmental decisions and actions)? If political participation is behavior, does it embrace all politically relevant activity (for example, race riots or steel strikes) or only activity that is designed to influence *governmental* authorities and decision-making? Are both legal and illegal activities to be viewed as political participation? Is any action directed to government decision-making to be regarded as participation, or only those actions that are effective? Do we include as political participation the action of individuals who contact government officials for help on individual or family problems (welfare, fixing a ticket)? Do we include activities organized by the government in support of itself? Actions taken out of fear or respect for someone the actor depends on (a landlord, village elder, union official, ward boss) or because the actor is paid, rather than because he seeks to influence governmental decision-making? Respected scholars differ on their answers to these questions.

In this essay, we define political participation simply as *activity by private citizens designed to influence governmental decision-making*. Several aspects of this core definition should be noted.

First, it includes activities but not attitudes. Some scholars, in contrast, define political participation so as to include the orientations of citizens towards politics, as well as their actual political behavior. We exclude this subjective component. Knowledge about politics, interest in politics, feelings of political competence and efficacy, perceptions of the relevance of politics, all these may often be closely related to political action, but at other times they are not. Their study and measurement also require techniques that differ significantly from those needed to study behavior alone. In our analysis, we are interested in how various attitudes and feelings are related to various forms of political action. We will thus treat objective political activity and subjective political attitudes as separate variables.

Second, we are concerned with the political activity of private citizens or, more precisely, of individuals in their roles as private citizens. We thus draw a distinction between political participants and political professionals. A political professional is someone whose primary calling is politics or government. Our concept of political participation excludes the activities of governmental officials, party officials, political candidates, and professional lobbyists acting in those roles. (It would not, for instance, encompass the activities of a high-level civil servant in determining governmental policy within his agency; it would include the activities of the civil servant in voting in an election or speaking at a town meeting.) The political activity of participants is intermittent, part-time, and usually avocational or secondary to other social roles. There is, thus, much political activity that is not political participation, including most of the activity of those who are most active in politics. The number, attitudes, and behavior of the political professionals, and particularly the political elite, in any particular political system, will often drastically affect the scope and nature of political participation—that is, nonprofessional activity—in that system. (See Chapter Two.)

Third, we are concerned only with activity that is designed to affect governmental decision-making. Such activity is focused on public authorities, those generally recognized as having the final legitimate decision on the authoritative allocation of values within the society. Much of what is often termed politics, and much of the allocation of resources among groups in society, may take place without intervention by government. Thus, a strike designed to influence the management of a private company to increase wages is not political participation by this definition; a strike designed to influence the government to increase ceilings on wages is political participation. And so also is a strike by sanitation men that is designed to induce a city council to pay higher wages. The amount of political participation in a society is thus, in some measure, a function of the scope of governmental activity in the society.

Efforts to influence governmental decision-making may involve persuading or pressuring existing authorities to act (or refrain from acting) in certain ways. Or participants may seek to replace current decision-makers with others whom they expect to be more responsive to their preferences and needs. More rarely, political participation may seek to change aspects of the political system itself, or to alter fundamentally the structure of the entire system, in order to make possible a government more responsive to the participants' desires. In short, political participation may be directed toward changing decisions by current authorities, toward replacing or retaining those authorities, or toward changing or defending the existing organization of the political system and the rules of the political game. All are means of influencing the decisions and the actions of the government.

Moreover, we define as political participation all activities that have these ends in mind, whether they are legal or illegal according to the established norms of the political system. Thus, protests, riots, demonstrations—even those forms of insurgent violence that are intended to influence the public authorities—are forms of political participation. To the extent that someone is engaged full-time, however, in illegal efforts to influence the government, he is one type of political professional—a professional revolutionary—and his activities are excluded, by definition, from participation.

Fourth, we include all activity that is designed to influence the government, whether or not it actually has that effect. This usage contrasts with that of some scholars, who include only successful efforts under the heading of political participation. In effect, they identify political participation with political power. For us, however, a participant in politics may or may not be successful and may or may not be powerful. A participant is successful to the extent that he actually influences those governmental decisions that he is attempting to influence. He is powerful according to the number and scope of the governmental decisions that he does actually influence and the degree of influence he has over those decisions. In these terms, most participants in politics have little power, and only some participants have a significant degree of success in politics. Widespread participation in politics thus does not necessarily imply democratic, responsible, or representative government.

Finally, we define political participation to include not only activity that is designed by the actor himself to influence governmental decision-making, but also activity that is designed by someone other than the actor to influence governmental decision-making. The former may be termed *autonomous* participation, the latter *mobilized* participation. The problem of intent, and the related question of the motivations for political participation, are complex and controversial.

Mobilized versus Autonomous Participation

Many of the people who vote, demonstrate, or take other actions that appear to be political participation do not act with the personal intention of influencing government decision-makers. Voting rates have been higher in traditional and rural eastern Turkey than in the more modernized western provinces or in the Turkish cities. But many of the peasants who swell the turnout vote because the local landlord tells them to do so; he may even threaten to take away their land if they do not follow his instructions. Some may have virtually no understanding of their action, much less an intent to affect the personnel or decisions of the government. A worker in Mexico City may join a PRI-sponsored demonstration not because he wants to display his support for the government and its decisions, but because he does not want to be different from all the other men in his factory. In America the nineteenth-century immigrant who put up campaign posters was not necessarily moved by clearly formulated views on the best candidate; he acted because the ward boss who had gotten him a job asked him to put up posters. In all these cases the immediate actor did not seek to influence government decision-making. But someone else—the landlord, the PRI union leader, the ward boss—did intend to do so. Through coercion, persuasion, or material inducements they were able to mobilize others in pursuit of their objectives.

Is mobilized participation to be regarded as political participation? Several studies have explicitly excluded mobilized or manipulated action from political participation. Thus, Myron Weiner stresses the voluntary nature of participation, arguing that "belonging to organizations or attending mass rallies under government orders is . . . excluded" as is voting in elections where citizens have no choice of candidates.[4] Another discussion of political participation does not attempt to define the term, but simply states the boundaries of the authors' interests. These explicitly rule out " 'ceremonial' or 'support' participation where citizens 'take part' by expressing support for the government, by marching in parades, by working hard in development projects, by participating in youth groups organized by the government, or by voting in ceremonial elections."[5] In both cases the writers distinguish democratic or autonomous participation from government-sponsored, manipulated, or mobilized participation, and exclude the latter from their definition.

We suggest that there are strong arguments for including both mobilized and autonomous categories in a broad-gauged exploration of patterns of political participation. First, the distinction between mobilized and autonomous participation is more clear-cut in principle than in reality. While it is possible to identify many activities as clearly mobilized or clearly autonomous, borderline cases abound. Moreover, the criteria for distinguishing the categories are somewhat arbitrary. Is support activity sponsored by the government mobilized, while action organized by opposition parties or organizations is autonomous? An individual's actions are about equally voluntary or involuntary in either a PRI-organized support demonstration or an opposition-oriented labor union that demands campaign contributions from its members. Clearly, much participation in democratic and competitive political systems contains some element of pressure and manipulation. Are the degree of real choice and the uncertainty of outcome in an election reliable criteria? How then does one compare the Soviet citizen, proud of his country and his party, who casts his vote in a single-ballot election, with the American voter, moved by a sense of civic duty and perhaps by partisan loyalty, who casts his ballot for a state official virtually guaranteed of re-election despite token opposition? In short, mobilized and autonomous participation are not clearly distinguished, dichotomous categories. Rather, they form a spectrum. The point on the spectrum that divides mobilized from autonomous participation is necessarily arbitrary. Precisely because the distinctions are arbitrary and the boundaries indistinct, we believe that both categories should be included in a research design, rather than an artificial line being drawn and all data and evidence on the far side of the boundary excluded.

Second, virtually all political systems include a mix of mobilized and autonomous participation. Of course, the mix varies from one system to another, and changes over time in any particular system. But we are dealing with matters of degree, not only at the level of individual actions but also at the level of political systems. The level of autonomous political participation is, for instance, typically higher in democratic political systems than it is in dictatorial systems. It would be a mistake, however, to conclude that there is no political participation in authoritarian or totalitarian systems. There is both autonomous and mobilized participation in such systems, although there may well be more of the latter than the former, and political participation obviously does not take the form of campaign activity and voting in competitive elections. Nondemocratic systems may well, however, have significant levels of collective lobbying, contacting, organizational activity, and violence. To restrict one's attention to autonomous political participation too easily leads to the erroneous assumption that political participation is a phenomenon unique to democratic politics.

A third reason for examining both mobilized and autonomous participation is the dynamic relation between the two categories. Behavior that originates as mobilized participation may become internalized, that is, largely autonomous. The immigrant who votes for the city machine initially because of gratitude to the boss may later become a convinced partisan, and argue vehemently that the machine's party is the best party for his class and for the nation. Similarly, voting in authoritarian systems, though originally motivated by fear of external pressure, may come to be a willing expression of civic duty, that is, an action designed to indicate support of the system and its leadership.

Conversely, initially autonomous participation may become mobilized or manipulated. Government and opposition parties and political leaders often try to infiltrate, "capture," and turn to their own interests local pressure organizations that were originally autonomous, such as neighborhood improvement associations in low-income urban areas. Why this attempt should succeed or fail, and how it affects members' participation patterns, can be explored only by investigating both the autonomous phase and the mobilized or manipulated phase.

A fourth reason for examining mobilized as well as autonomous activities is that both have important consequences for the political system. Both mobilized and autonomous participation offer opportunities for leadership and provide constraints on political leaders. A political

No Easy Choice

leader who can mobilize supporters is in a very different position from one who cannot, and his actions have very different consequences for the political system. In this respect, the consequences of the actions of political leaders with mobilized support and those with autonomous support are likely to resemble each other more than either resembles the consequences of the actions of political leaders who lack both mobilized and autonomous support. To say that a mobilized, as distinguished from autonomous, actor does not participate in politics is like saying that a conscripted, as distinguished from volunteer, soldier does not participate in a war. The motivations of the two are clearly different and, in some respects, their behavior may be different. But the great bulk of the activities of the conscript and the volunteer in a war will be indistinguishable from each other and will have similar consequences. The same is true of the actions and impact of mobilized and autonomous participants in politics, despite their different motives.

Levels, Forms, and Bases of Political Participation

The basic purpose of this study is to analyze the effects of social and economic modernization on political participation. Thus, political participation is our overall dependent variable. We will attempt to shed some light on how various changes associated with modernization affect patterns of participation: the level of various types of participation, the mixture of forms of participation, and the changing group bases for participation.

In all societies some people participate in politics. In some societies more people participate in politics than in other societies. In any society some people participate more than other people. Consider, for instance, the following figures on levels of political participation:[6]

(1) Percentages of adult population voting in a national election (mid-1960s):

Bulgaria	100.0%	India	55.8%
Austria	88.9	Chile	54.1
Venezuela	78.8	Brazil	44.2
United Kingdom	72.4	Guatemala	25.9
Turkey	61.2	Switzerland	23.2
United States	56.8	South Africa	14.3

(2) Percentage of the population which engages in one or more political acts beyond voting (1966-1969):

	Number of political acts beyond voting					
	1	2	3	4	5	6
United States	64%	40%	26%	16%	9%	5%
Japan	62	35	19	11	5	2
Nigeria	56	30	13	2	1(5+)	-
Austria	52	41	17	8	4	2
India	36	18	10	6	4	2

(3) Percentage of population which is "political active," that is, discusses politics once a week or engages in more intense political activity (1959-1960):

United States	46%
Great Britain	45
Germany	40
Italy	27
Mexico	25

These cross-national data on participation levels reveal many similarities and differences. Voting is a widespread phenomenon in the most widely disparate societies. In many societies other types of political activity above and beyond voting are also widely engaged in: in industrialized countries 50% or more of the population participate in ways other than voting; even in an underdeveloped country like India, more than one-third of the population does more than vote. On the other hand, there are also significant differences among societies in voting rates and participation rates and in the meanings of those rates. There are also, clearly, major differences within societies. In each country, a minority of political activists can easily be distinguished from the bulk of the population. At the other extreme, in every society at least one-third of the population engages in no political activity beyond voting, and in some countries, such as the United States, over one-third may not even bother to vote.

In analyzing levels of participation, it is necessary to distinguish between two sub-dimensions: (a) *scope*, or the proportion of a defined category of people who engage in a particular participatory activity; and (b) *intensity*, or the scale, duration, and importance of the particular activity for the political system. By and large, the scope and intensity of political participation tend to be inversely related. In a given society, large numbers of people may vote, an action of little intensity; smaller numbers of people may participate in campaign activities; and still smaller numbers may play a continuing role individually and through organizations in attempting to influence government decisions.

Political participation takes many different forms. Studies of participation may use slightly varying classification schemes, but most recent research distinguishes among the following types of behavior.

(a) *Electoral activity* includes voting, but also campaign contributions, working in an election, proselytizing on behalf of a candidate, or any other action designed to affect the outcome of the electoral process. Voting is much more widespread than other forms of political participation, and hence the factors associated with its incidence often distinguish it from other types of participation, including other campaign activity.[7] There is, nonetheless, an interrelated cluster of activity that is focused about the electoral cycle and voting and is clearly distinguishable from other major forms of political action.

(b) *Lobbying* includes individual or group efforts to contact governmental officials and political leaders with a view to influencing their decisions on issues that affect a significant number of people. Obvious instances are activity designed to generate support or opposition for a particular legislative proposal or administrative decision.

(c) *Organizational activity* involves participation as a member or officer in an organization that has as its primary and explicit goal the influencing of government decision-making. Such organizations may focus their efforts on highly specialized interests or may address a wide spectrum of public issues. Being a member of such an organization constitutes in itself a form of political participation, whether or not one takes part in the organization's efforts to influence government. Inactive membership is, in a sense, participation by proxy.

(d) *Contacting* is individual action directed to government officials and normally designed to produce benefits for only a single person or a very small number of people. Here we follow Verba, Nie, and Kim, who found that "particularized contacting" is a mode of political participation separate from and almost wholly unrelated to other modes.[8]

Electoral activity, lobbying, organizational activity, and contacting all may take legal or illegal forms. Bribery, intimidation, and falsification of electoral results, to the extent that they are engaged in by private citizens rather than professionals, are as clearly political participation as are voting, attending party rallies, or putting up campaign posters. Lobbying activities such as peaceful strikes, demonstrations, and picketing are legal in some countries and barred elsewhere. Similarly, private contacting can be legal or illegal in itself, and may or may not be accompanied by bribery or other illegal aspects.

Crossing the boundary between legal and illegal activity involves greater risk and hence greater initiative by the participant. One might expect a screening effect that would be similar to that between those who vote and the smaller and less broadly representative number of electoral activists who engage in campaign efforts. But many kinds of illegal political participation are simply the extension of legal efforts to influence government decision-makers. In addition, the line between legal and illegal activity varies from one country to another and may change over time in any one country.

(e) *Violence* can also be a form of political participation, and it is useful analytically to define it as a distinct category: that is, as efforts to affect governmental decision-making by doing physical damage to persons or property. Except in certain instances, where it is employed by police or law enforcement agencies, such action is illegal in every society. A resort to violence, consequently, usually reflects fairly intense motivations. Violence may be directed at changing the political leadership (coups d'etat, asassinations), affecting governmental policies (riots, revolts), or changing the entire political system (revolution). Each of these goals, of course, may also be pursued by peaceful means. Hence, a central issue is under what conditions do people resort to violence rather than to more peaceful forms of participation? To what extent does violent action tend to be a last resort, chosen only after opportunities for peaceful participation have disappeared? To what extent is violence more likely to be used by some social forces than others? And under what circumstances does it tend to be closely associated with other types of participation? [9]

Most studies of political participation have focused on levels of participation and, more specifically, on the level of voting participation. In societies where there is a history of competitive elections, election statistics, census data, and sample surveys make it easy and interesting to compare the voting turnout of different groups and different societies. Voting participation, however, is clearly only one form of participation, even in societies where voting is frequent and meaningful. One should not, consequently, assume that because one group votes less than another, therefore its other forms of political participation are less. They may be, but they do not necessarily have to be. Similarly, it would be erroneous to assume that because voting participation goes up in a society other forms of political participation have also increased.

Nor is there any easy way to measure the scope and intensity of various forms of participation, weight them in some manner, and add them into a composite index that measures "total participation." Such an index would be meaningful only if all forms of participation had similar characteristics, in the sense that each increased or decreased in response to the same causal variables and had similar consequences for the political system as a whole. But all forms of political participation do not have similar characteristics. Some types cluster together. Far more people vote than contribute funds or actively campaign for a candidate. Electoral activity as a whole has some characteristics similar to lobbying. But particularized contacting displays rather different characteristics. In each of the several nations where it has been examined, the scope or incidence of contacting does not vary systematically with socio-economic level as do most other forms of participation. Moreover, the consequences for the political system (and indirectly for social and economic change) vary with different patterns of participation. A pattern where many people vote and contact but few lobby would have different effects than a pattern where voting turnouts are low but lobbying is widespread and intense. We cannot simply add up the incidence of different forms of participation and arrive at a meaningful number.

In other words, if we want to understand the causes and consequences of different patterns of political participation, we cannot think of participation as a simple, homogenous variable. *"Political participation" is an umbrella concept, a label for a whole set of variables; each variable fits the core definition, but each also has somewhat different causes and consequences and relates differently to social and economic trends.* Only in the most general sense, then, can we speak of an over-all increase in the level of political participation in a society, or conclude that country A has a higher level of participation than country B. Nonetheless, it is possible to perceive gross changes and contrasts, and we will, at times, talk in terms of changes in overall participation levels.

In different societies, political participation may be rooted in different group bases. Except for contacting, most political participation involves some form of collaborative activity and has benefits for some form of collectivity. It is, consequently, possible to analyze participation in terms of the different types of collective organizations through which participation is organized and which commonly form the bases for such participation. Among the more common bases are:

(a) *class*: individuals of similar social status, income, and occupation;

(b) *communal group:* individuals of similar race, religion, language, or ethnicity;

(c) *neighborhood:* individuals residing in geographical proximity to each other;

(d) *party*: individuals who identify with the same formal organization attempting to win or maintain control of the executive and legislative branches of government; and

(e) *faction*: individuals united by sustained or intense personal interaction with each other, one manifestation of which is the *patron-client grouping*, that is, a faction involving the reciprocal exchange of benefits between individuals of unequal status, wealth, and influence.

Much of the discussion about political participation centers on the relative importance of these various bases for organizing participation and how the bases relate to each other. Students of Africa, for instance, debate the relative importance of class and communal grouping in shaping political participation. In some societies, class and party identifications closely correlate with each other; in others, they cross-cut each other.

The Causes of Participation

The most interesting and relevant questions for analysis have to do with the shifting patterns of participation. How do the major economic and social changes associated with modernization affect the scope or incidence of different forms of political participation in a society? Does the mix of forms and of bases change in any systematic way? How do the forms and levels of participation directed at local levels of government relate to, and compare with, those directed at national government? How is this balance affected by social and economic change?

In theory, the tendency of individuals and groups to try to influence the government is affected by their access to alternative means of pursuing their goals. If nonpolitical means are as promising as, or more promising than, political channels, people may be expected to invest their time and energy accordingly. For some problems, the government is inherently the sole or most obvious remedy. If a local or national government makes a decision that is viewed as harmful to the interests of certain groups, the most obvious course is to try to persuade the government to alter its decision. The government is the source of the difficulty and hence is its most direct (though not necessarily most promising) solution. Where ethnic tensions focus on questions of relative status and power, they are likely to take a political form. Other issues—promoting individual and family welfare, improving neighborhood facilities, coping with the effects of a drought—may or may not prompt individuals or groups to turn to governmental action, depending on the perceived availability and effectiveness of this course compared with alternative means.

In the following chapters we will attempt to probe the relationship between socio-economic change and changes in the levels, forms, and bases of political participation. In Chapter Two, we will analyse political participation in relation to the other goals that confront societies and their political elites, emphasizing that political participation is not, in most cases, highly valued in and of itself. In Chapter Three, these choices are examined at the macro level: how the overall economic and political characteristics of the society—its level of economic development and its degree of economic equality—are related to its level and forms of political participation. In Chapter Four, we will shift to the micro level and explore the relative impact of social status, mobility opportunities, and organizational context on the choices of individuals to participate or not to participate in politics. Chapter Five, in turn, shifts to what might be called the "mecro" or group level and focuses specifically on the problems of participation by low-income groups. In the final chapter, we attempt to pull together the themes and conclusions that have emerged from our analysis and suggest what they imply for the prospects of broadened participation in the developing nations.

Goals and Choices: Participation in the Context of Development

Models of Development

Political participation is valued differently in different societies. Where it is thought to be a desirable goal, the expansion of political participation involves costs and trade-offs in terms of other goals, and these costs and trade-offs will vary in different societies at different levels of overall modernization or development.* In this chapter, we will attempt to sketch out, in a preliminary way, some of the relationships between political participation and other aspects of development. We will be concerned, first, with political participation in relation to the overall choices confronting societies and, then, with political participation as a goal or antigoal from the viewpoint of political elites. The major point is that the role of political participation in a society is a function of the priorities accorded to other variables and goals and of the overall strategy of development, if any, that the leadership of the society has adopted.

American society is unique in the extraordinarily high value it places

*We will use the words "modernization" or "development" to refer to the overall processes of social, economic, intellectual, political, and cultural change that are associated with the movement of societies from relatively poor, rural, agrarian conditions to relatively affluent, urban, industrialized conditions. Our usage is comparable to that of Cyril E. Black, *The Dynamics of Modernization* (New York: Harper and Row, 1966). We will use the phrase "socio-economic development" to refer to those portions of this overall process that involve urbanization, industrialization, commercialization of agriculture, media and communications development, diversification of the occupational structure, and related processes, which are often subsumed under the two concepts "economic development" and "social mobilization." See Samuel P. Huntington, *Political Order in Changing Societies* (New Haven: Yale University Press, 1968), pp. 33-34. We will use the phrase "economic growth" to refer to the increase in overall economic wealth of a society as measured, typically, by per capita gross domestic product.

on high levels of autonomous political participation. Private citizens feel guilty when they do not vote (to the extent that 5% to 10% claim they did vote when they did not), and public officials deplore low turnouts and appoint commissions to investigate their causes. People are expected to take an active part in local community affairs, PTAs, labor unions, churches, and other associations. Those who do so elicit by and large the at-least-grudging respect of those who do not. The heritage of individual involvement in public affairs, which came over on the Mayflower, was reinforced by the necessities of a frontier existence and by the concept of popular sovereignty. The Jacksonian idea that every citizen is capable of discharging the normal functions of government is a peculiarly American one in the modern world: Political involvement is good for society—it makes democracy more meaningful and government more responsive—and it is good for the individual—it develops him as a moral being and as a responsible citizen of society. This belief manifests itself not only in the number and frequency of elections for public officials, but also in the number and activity of the many associations that are formed to promote private interests and the public good. In de Tocqueville's oft-quoted words: "Americans of all ages, all conditions, and all dispositions constantly form associations. They have not only commercial and manufacturing companies, in which all take part, but associations of a thousand other kinds, religious, moral, serious, futile, general or restricted, enormous or dimunitive . . . Wherever at the head of some new undertaking you can see the government in France, or a man of rank in England, in the United States you will be sure to find an association."

Given this heritage, it is not surprising that Americans should believe that the expansion of political participation is a desirable goal for other societies as well as their own. Nor is it surprising that they should believe that its achievement is tied in with the attainment of other desirable social goals, or that the American Congress should write this goal into legislation specifying the ends and conditions of American economic assistance to other societies. And it is not surprising that Americans should be slow to realize the extent to which their beliefs and practices concerning political participation are in so many respects irrelevant or inapplicable to other societies.

The prevalent American attitude toward political participation is reflected in the liberal model of development, which was implicitly or explicitly articulated in much of the American and other writing on this subject in the 1950s and 1960s. In this model, it was assumed that the causes of socio-economic inequality, political violence, and lack of democratic political participation lay in the socio-economic backwardness of a society. The answer to these ills, consequently, was rapid socioeconomic modernization and development, which would increase the overall level of economic well-being in the society and thus make possible a more equitable distribution of wealth, promote political stability, and provide the basis for broader political participation and more democratic systems of government. The causal relationships most commonly assumed to underlie this model are diagrammed in Figure 2.1.

The empirical basis for the liberal model was found in the seeming correlations between socio-economic backwardness, on the one hand, and the evils of inequality, instability, and arbitrary rule, on the other. Gunnar Myrdal expressed the prevailing view about the relation between socio-economic backwardness and inequality when he argued that, "It is, indeed, a regular occurrence endowed almost with the dignity of an economic law that the poorer the country, the greater the difference between rich and poor."[1] Robert McNamara succinctly summarized the lesson from the statistics of civil strife when he declared that "there is an irrefutable relationship between violence and economic backwardness."[2] Seymour Martin Lipset and Daniel Lerner presented comparative data to demonstrate the positive relation between economic development and democracy, in the one case, and socio-economic modernization and political participation, in the other.[3]

Figure 2.1   The "Benign Line" of the Liberal Model

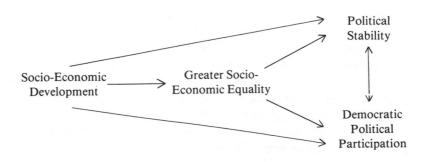

In the past decade the liberal model of development has been shown to be methodologically weak, empirically questionable, and historically irrelevant, except under specialized circumstances. Three methodological weaknesses characterized the model. First, its assumptions about causal relationships were, in large part, derived from aggregate static comparisons between the most developed (i.e., Western European and North Atlantic) countries, on the one hand, and the great bulk of the less developed countries, on the other, without recognizing that further differentiation among countries might invalidate the presumed linear relationship between socio-economic development and other variables. A second and related weakness was that the model ignored the impact that the processes of changing from one developmental level to another might have on the dependent variables of stability, equity, and participation. A third general weakness was the jump that was often made from correlated data to presumed causal relationships. The liberal model rested, in large part, on what can only be described as a neo-Marxist premise: that the causal flow would be from economics to politics rather than in the reverse direction.

During the past decade several of the model's individual causal relationships have also been challenged and have been discarded or drastically modified. Political violence and instability have been shown to be more prevalent in societies in the midst of the process of modernization and development than in societies at the lowest levels of development.[4] In a similar vein, it has come to be accepted that, with the notable exception of societies that have carried out extensive land reform programs, societies in the middle phases of socio-economic development tend to have less equal distributions of income than societies that are either much less developed or much more developed. In addition, high rates of economic growth are often associated with increasing inequalities in income and property distribution in modernizing countries. Typical of the conclusions of economists on the relationship between these two variables are those of Adelman and Morris: "Higher rates of industrialization, faster increases in agricultural productivity, and higher rates of growth all tend to shift the income distribution in favor of the higher income groups and against the low income groups. The dynamics of the process of economic development tend to work relatively against the poor; the major recipients of the rewards of economic development are consistently the middle class and the highest income groups.''[5] The connection between economic development and democracy has also been questioned in a lengthy series of static comparisons and developmental studies. The general import of these studies is to shift the explanatory emphasis from simple affluence to economic equality and developmental sequences.[6]

In actual practice, very few countries, if any, apart from the United States, have approximated the liberal model of development. Other societies have, by and large, valued political participation less and have had to pay more to get it, by the sacrifice of other goals. For contemporary developing countries, a variety of alternative models seem more useful in relating political participation to other developmental variables. In particular, four models—which we will label bourgeois, autocratic, populist, and technocratic—seem to us to capture the dynamic changes among these variables in many contemporary cases. We do not mean to suggest that these four models are the only possibilities, in logic or in fact. Some countries are better described in terms of a "low-level steady-state" model characterized by very little participation or growth, fragile stability, and an equity reflecting widely shared poverty rather than effective redistribution. Successful revolutionary regimes offer still another model, featuring very rapid expansion of participation and radical redistribution of incomes and wealth, although at later stages the tensions between economic growth and socio-economic equity manifest themselves. But successful revolutions are rare, and the low-level steady state offers little to analyze. The four models we discuss are helpful in analyzing how participation relates to other key developmental variables in many of the nations that have broken out of the low-level steady-state, but have not experienced a successful revolution.

In such nations, relations among participation and other developmental variables are likely to change during different phases in the evolution of overall levels of political participation. A first phase concerns the expansion of political participation to the urban middle class; in the second phase, the issue is the expansion of political participation to the urban and rural lower classes. In Phase I, economic development begins to get underway, economic inequality increases, particularly in the countryside, and the socio-economic basis for the expansion of political participation begins to emerge. At this point, the society is confronted with, in effect, a choice between what may be termed the "bourgeois" and "autocratic" models of development. Should priority be given to the political needs of the emerging urban middle class or to the economic needs of the declining rural peasantry? If the bourgeois model is followed, political participation is expanded to encompass the urban middle class and economic growth proceeds reasonably rapidly. Economic inequality also increases, both as a concomitant of economic growth and as a result of the utilization by the middle class of its political power to further its own ends. The development of electoral and parliamentary institutions that provide channels for political participation by the bourgeois-middle class groups also helps to promote at least short-run political stability. The expansion of political participation is limited to the expanding middle class, and, over time, the middle class expands more slowly as a result of the economic inequality produced by economic growth and the expansion of political participation. In due course, the more general processes of socio-economic development have their effects on the lower classes; these classes become socially mobilized, and they begin to demand opportunities for political participation and access to political power. At this point, the system moves into Phase II and is confronted with a choice between the "technocratic" or "populist" models of development.

Alternatively, in Phase I a society may approximate the autocratic model of development, in which power is concentrated, political participation by the middle class is suppressed, economic growth is enhanced, and socio-economic equality may be promoted as a way of securing the support of the lower classes against the middle classes. In promoting this equality, the basic issue is usually whether governmental authorities can use the power of the state to impose an effective land reform on a traditional aristocracy that will oppose it, an embryonic urban middle class that is indifferent to it, and a peasantry that can do little to promote it. If the government is able to bring about such a reform, the trend towards economic inequality produced by economic growth will be reversed, and a substantial class of small rural landholders may emerge. The achievement of this result requires a concentration of power and an effective bureaucratic implementation of policy, and these are often beyond the political capacities of governments in developing countries. If, however, the system does move in this direction, short-run political stability may also be achieved so long as the urban middle classes can be effectively excluded from politics. This stability may be challenged by middle class groups (such as the officer corps) who are in a strategic position to demand some form of effective political participation in addition to the opportunities for individual mobility and personal enrichment that economic growth may offer. In the longer run, the political system will be challenged by lower classes, who, having benefited from land reform or other measures promoting socio-economic equality, come to seek more meaningful access to the political system. At this point the autocratic model, like the bourgeois model, is confronted with the Phase II problem of whether and how to provide for lower-class political participation.

One response to this challenge is the technocratic model of development, characterized by low levels of political participation, high levels of investment (particularly foreign investment) and economic growth, and increasing income inequalities. This model assumes that political participation must be held down, at least temporarily, in order to promote economic development, and that such development necessarily involves at least temporary increases in income inequality. The unanswered question is: To what extent is increasing income inequality compatible with sustained low levels of political participation? Will not a widening gap between rich and poor, combined with governmental efforts to repress political participation, build up stresses and pressures and lead eventually to a "participation explosion," which will overthrow the existing political system and may alter fundamentally the social and economic structure? Does not departicipation-growth-inequality-repression constitute a vicious circle, the dynamics of which tend to shift initiative and power to those who want to carry the process to the extreme?

The causal sequence in the populist model of development is almost the reverse of that in the technocratic model. High and increasing levels of political participation go with expanding governmental benefits and welfare policies, increasing economic equality, and, if necessary, relatively low rates of economic growth. The logic of this pattern of evolution leads toward increasing social conflict and the polarization of society, as more groups become participant and attempt to share in a stagnant, or only slowly growing, economic pie. Thus, while the technocratic model leads to governmental repression in order to prevent political participation, the populist model leads to civil strife as a result

No Easy Choice

of political participation. In both cases, and in a comparable manner, the dynamics of the relationships among the critical variables tend to produce a vicious circle in which the dominant tendencies are toward the maximization of the value of each variable. While the strains generated by the technocratic model may eventually lead to a participation explosion, those that arise in the populist model may eventually lead either to the total disruption of the society by civil war or to a "participation implosion," in which the military seize power and suppress participation by other social forces. If they remain in power, the military leaders may well attempt to redirect society into the technocratic pattern; if they withdraw from power, the society is likely to resume another cycle in the populist pattern.

This differentiation between Phase I and Phase II, and between the bourgeois and autocratic models of Phase I and the populist and technocratic models of Phase II, suggests that the relation between political participation and other developmental goals is much more complex than is assumed by the liberal model. In Phase I, a conflict exists between the expansion of political participation and the achievement of greater socioeconomic equality. In Phase II, a conflict exists between the expansion of political participation and more rapid economic growth. In both phases, developmental strategies may well give higher priority to goals other than political participation and may well attempt to reduce political participation in order to achieve those goals. In both phases, also, the attitudes of key elites toward political participation are quite likely to be functions of

Figure 2.2 The "Vicious Circle" of the Technocratic Model

Figure 2.3   The "Vicious Circle" of the Populist Model

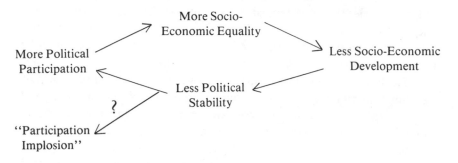

their attitudes towards those other goals. Thus, in Phase I, more participation is compatible with growth but not with equity; in Phase II, more participation is compatible with equity but not with growth.

Unlike the liberal model, these other four models all assume at least some incompatibility among the possible goals of development. In addition, unlike the liberal model, all four models also assign a more important role to political participation as an independent as well as a dependent variable. In both phases, the expansion or restriction of political participation affects the degree of socio-economic equality. In Phase II, indeed, political elites in both populist and technocratic systems recognize the conflict between equity and growth, and their choices between these two goals shape their attitudes towards the expansion or restriction of political participation.

Like the liberal model, all four additional models are, of course, ideal types. Some countries, however, have closely approximated one ideal or the other, and other countries have veered strongly in one direction or the other, or from one direction to the other. In the 1950s and 1960s Iran and Taiwan, for instance, tended towards the autocratic model; Colombia and, after 1973, Thailand had many characteristics of the bourgeois model, while Peru in the late 1960s seemed to shift from the latter to the former. In somewhat similar fashion, in the late 1950s and early 1960s, Brazil evolved along classically populist lines, a pattern that was brought to an end by the military coup d'etat of 1964 and subsequent participation implosion, which, in due course, transformed

Brazil into a close approximation of the technocratic model. In the late 1960s and early 1970s, Brazil stood in dramatic contrast to Chile, which, until 1973, represented a close approximation of the populist model. Other countries that have tended in the populist direction, at one time or another, are India, Sri Lanka, Tanzania, and Uruguay. In contrast to them, countries like Indonesia, the Ivory Coast, Kenya, and Spain under Franco tended to move in a technocratic direction.

The liberal model of development avoided the problem of choice by claiming that all desirable values could be maximized. But it has turned out not to be a realistic or relevant choice for most modernizing countries. They are, instead, forced to choose some variant of the other models. The choice that a society's elite makes reflects its own basic moral and political values, of course, and any choice can be rationalized and legitimized in terms of political ideology, social theory, and economic analysis. These differing perspectives can interpret the same experience in different ways, as Henry Bienen points out in his discussion of Kenya:

> Kenya together with the Ivory Coast have been to some observers signal "success stories" after independence. Kenya, like the Ivory Coast, has had more than a respectable rate of growth in gross domestic product. Both countries have had neighbors to contrast them to. *Ghana and the Ivory Coast* is already the title of a book. *Kenya and Tanzania* is sure to follow and the comparisons between the two East African countries are already many. And both Kenya and the Ivory Coast have opted for seemingly clear strategies of economic growth based on a determination to keep ties to Western countries and gain foreign aid and investment; both have concentrated on growth rather than redistribution. Both countries have been controlled by a "maximum leader" and a small group around him who have strong ethnic ties. Indeed, both countries could be characterized by an attitude among the ruling group of "benevolent elitism."

On the other hand, those committed to a populist model put a different gloss on the Kenyan experience:

> Some observers would say that the elitism is not so benevolent. . . . They are seen to be countries where neo-colonial influence is strong

and where a parasitical elite of top politicians and civil servants squeeze the rural areas for their ill-gotten gains. They are seen to be without ideology. . . . Growth takes place at the expense of the poor: the rich get richer and the poor stagnate or worse. A privileged elite distributes the benefits of economic growth that it gains through alliances with Europeans and through expropriation of Africans and Asians to tribal clients unfettered by any of the formal mechanisms of control which reside in the Legislature and elections. . . . This same elite arrogates to itself the wisdom to choose a path for development on the grounds that people do not understand developmental problems and will, if left to themselves, allocate resources on a short run calculation for schools, clinics, roads, and other immediate benefits. Curtailing effective mass participation is thus justified. Organized dissent is not allowed and the heavy hand of civil administration and, if need be, police and riot squads are used to put down opposition.[7]

All the models posit certain relationships between political participation, socio-economic development, socio-economic equality, and political stability. As has been pointed out, the liberal model's assumptions about the relations between socio-economic development and political stability, and between socio-economic development and socio-economic equality, have been shown not to be well founded. The next chapter will explore in general terms the relations between socio-economic development and political participation, and between socio-economic equality and political participation. The evidence from the Harvard Project, as well as from other sources, shows that the liberal model's assumptions about these relationships need not be totally discarded, although they do have to be considerably refined. Socio-economic development and participation do, in large measure, go together, but the connection between them is more complex and ambiguous than it is often assumed to be. Equality and participation are closely connected but the causal flow seems to be as much from the latter to the former (as posited by the other models) as from the former to the latter (as assumed by the liberal model). In addition, the liberal model generally appears to overemphasize the effects of social and economic factors on participation. At least in the short run, the values of the political elite and the policies of government are more decisive than anything else in shaping the participation patterns of a society.

No Easy Choice

The Choices of Political Elites

In any given society at any given moment, the levels, bases, and forms of political participation are shaped to a far greater degree by politics than by anything else. Yet, in the analysis of the factors shaping political participation, it is striking that politics has either been ignored or relegated to a secondary position in comparison with the extensive treatment accorded social, economic, and cultural forces. The latter obviously influence the general context and environment in which decisions about participation are made, but, in the final analysis, the most decisive influences are those that stem from the political values and traditions of the society, the nature of its political institutions, and the sources, nature, and goals of its political leadership.

The attitude of the political elites towards political participation is, in any society, probably the single most decisive factor influencing the nature of participation in that society. Mobilized participation occurs only when political elites make efforts to involve masses of the population in politics. Autonomous participation can occur at reasonable costs only if political elites encourage it, permit it, or are unable or unwilling to suppress it. Over the long term, changes in the social, economic, and demographic configuration of a society will alter the nature of its political participation. The changes so generated, however, will often be effected through changes in the composition or goals of the political elites. The changes that occur within any given five-year period occur only because the political elite changes its attitudes towards political participation, or because it is itself replaced or challenged by a different elite with different attitudes toward participation.

In traditional societies, political participation is usually not highly valued. Both elite and mass accept the inevitability, if not the positive desirability, of deference, hierarchy, and the existing order of people and things. In many, if not most, of the poorer countries, the expansion of political participation is not, in fact, a widely held goal. Many social scientists, including ourselves in this essay, at times discuss the obstacles to the expansion of political participation in developing countries by focusing primarily on the more visible, external, or objective barriers to that expansion. In actuality, however, the crucial barriers are internal and subjective. They are the beliefs of political elites and private citizens that the expansion of political participation is not a goal that it is in their interest to promote and may well be a goal that it is in their interest consciously to avoid or to oppose. Americans may deplore this attitude. But they should recognize that the perception of political participation as an antigoal is usually rooted in a realistic appraisal, by elites and other citizens, of their own interests, in terms of social, economic, and political conditions prevailing in many poor countries.

Modernizing elites almost always publicly espouse and articulate the desirability of more widespread political participation, but the extent to which this general attitude is reflected in actions and policies varies greatly. Most political elites undoubtedly would like to have the benefits of widespread participation, in terms of support for themselves and their policies, but would not like to pay the costs for that participation, in terms of limits on their power, the time and effort required to win acquiescence, and the demands that participation produces for the allocation of scarce resources. For most political elites political participation is, at best, an instrumental rather than a primary value. Their attitude about the desirable levels, forms, and bases of participation will be determined in large part by the effects these have on their ability:

(a) to get into power and to remain in power; and

(b) to achieve other social, economic, and political goals, such as national independence, revolutionary change, economic development, and socio-economic equality.

Power

Political elites out of power are more likely to be interested in expanding political participation, changing its bases, and, at times, developing new forms of participation. Bringing new actors into the political arena is a classic way of altering the balance of power in that arena. Yet the ability of political elites who are not in control of the government actually to accomplish this is usually limited. The more decisive influences on political participation come from those elites who are able to command the offices and resources of government. These dominant political elites normally are unsympathetic to the expansion of political participation. While they may be in a position to broaden the scope of political participation for their own benefit, they are much more inclined to see any shift in the participation pattern as a threat to the political status quo, of which they are the principal beneficiaries. Thus, those who have the capability to expand political participation often lack the interest to do so; those who have the interest often lack the capability.

In order to maintain themselves in power, political elites may act to restrict competition and thereby lower the level of political participation. As a matter of course, autocratic and technocratic regimes limit political freedoms and suppress political participation. A "participation implosion," such as occurred in Brazil in 1964, has suppression as a primary purpose and a primary consequence. Elites that are willing to use more direct and coercive methods can, of course, apply a variety of threats, administrative controls, and physical sanctions to reduce participation levels. This repression can, on the one hand, take the relatively "mild" form of imposing illegal or semilegal restrictions on the activities of opposition political parties and leaders. In Kenya, for instance:

> In 1968, Government refused to allow fair municipal elections to take place. The then existing opposition party, KPU, had its candidates barred through administrative procedures. It was claimed that they had made out their papers incorrectly when filing. It was the regional administration which acted as the agent for squashing the possibilities of free elections and a number of district commissioners were unhappy about the political use made of them.[8]

At the extreme, direct force and violence may also be used against actual or potential participants. In both Mexico City and Lima, governmental repression of protest activities by the poor tended to have a very substantial deterrent impact on the propensity of these groups to engage in subsequent protest activity and, indeed, to have much interest at all in politics.[9] In autocratic and technocratic societies, effective political participation is generally limited to elite factions operating within the inner precincts of the political system, and to counterelite factions operating outside the system and attempting to destroy it.

Within more democratic systems, voting participation is significantly affected by the intensity and nature of electoral and party competition in the society. In the United States after 1896, for example, a realignment of social forces led to a drastic decline in party competition, as both southern and northern states tended to become one-party. Voting participation declined steadily from a high in 1896 of approximately 80%

of the eligible electorate, to less than 50% in 1924. Interestingly, voter turnout remained high in the border states, where party competition remained close. In the 1950s the differences in voting turnout among American states (running from an average of 64.6% in Idaho to 4.2% in Mississippi) showed an extremely high correlation (Spearman rank order, .807) with the degree of party competition in the states.[10]

The intensity of competition is affected not only by the distribution of support among competing parties but also by the number of parties. In a multiparty system, each party tends to mobilize its own constituency rather than to compete with another party to win the support of a wavering constituency. Direct competition among the parties is less than it would be in a two-party system and, consequently, voting participation rates should, other things being equal, also be lower. Evidence from state and national elections in India supports this proposition.[11]

Political elites who wish to maintain themselves in power by reducing political participation may achieve this objective by limiting the intensity of political competition in their society. In Colombia, for instance, in 1958, after the ouster of the populist dictator Rojas Pinilla, the leaders of the two traditional parties consciously attempted to lower the levels of political activity in their society by eliminating, so far as possible, electoral competition. They agreed to form a National Front for sixteen years, under which the Presidency would alternate between the two parties and the seats in Congress would be allocated between them. The result was a steady decline in voting turnout until 1970, when the presence of a strong anti-National Front candidate (Rojas Pinilla) produced both a close election and a marked increase in turnout. The proportion of the adult population voting in presidential elections was as follows:[12]

1958	50.4%
1962	38.2
1966	34.2
1970	46.4

While the normal tendency of political elites in power is to restrict political participation, there are circumstances where governmental leaders may follow a different course and attempt to mobilize new groups politically in order to bolster their power. Some of the most significant

No Easy Choice

expansions of political participation have, indeed, taken place precisely under those circumstances where interest and capability coincide.

Every political leader or group of political leaders, even in completely nondemocratic systems, has to have some group or groups that are his source of strength and support, that are, in some sense, "his people," his constituency, those whom he can rely on because of mutual and reciprocal interests. Political participation expands most dramatically when a political leader seizes upon the possibility of incorporating into the political arena some new group, not formerly participant, and thus creating a new base for his own power. The development of such a new political base or constituency is, indeed, one mark of an outstanding political leader.

A political leader may mobilize a new constituency before he comes into power and utilize that mobilization as the means of winning power. To do this, however, often runs the risk of directly challenging and frightening the established elite and provoking a confrontation and possible repression. The successful "constituency creator" is more likely to come into power through accepted means and as a result of support from the accepted political participants. Once in power, however, he may then utilize his control of the machinery of the state to shift his basis of support and, usually, to broaden it by mobilizing and organizing one or more new constituencies. Thus, Cárdenas came to power in Mexico as the personal choice of Calles and the revolutionary oligarchy; once in power, however, he turned on his patron, disassociated himself from the older generation of revolutionary generals, and mobilized new sources of support among workers and peasant groups for himself and the revolutionary party. In Argentina, Perón came to power as a result of a military coup, but then shifted his political base from the army to the urban workers and lower middle classes, organizing these groups as effective participants in the political arena. So also, in Turkey, Menderes was originally elected to office largely as a result of urban opposition to the Republican Peoples Party, but he then directed governmental policies toward the rural sector, in order to overcome the bifurcation that had existed in Turkish politics and mobilize the peasantry into politics as a solid base of support for his party. "What does it matter what the intellectuals in Istanbul think," as he put it, "so long as the peasantry is with us?"[13]

In these cases, the political leaders were relatively successful in mobilizing new groups into politics and creating effective power bases for themselves. In other cases, the outcomes may be different, either because of the inherent difficulty in mobilizing a group or because the group has already been partly mobilized by other political leaders. The Shah of Iran tried to use land reform to mold the peasantry into an effective constituency for the monarchy; his efforts suffered from the overall low level of social mobilization of the peasantry and, hence, the difficulty of changing them into an effective political force. President Thieu's attempts to use land reform for the same purposes were, on the other hand, restricted by the extent to which the peasantry had already been mobilized by the Viet Cong.

The introduction into politics of a new group, and its effective use by a political leader as a power base, normally involves action on four fronts:

(a) the use of governmental policy to benefit the group;

(b) the organization of the group through functional associations, political parties, or some other means;

(c) the creation of new structural (often electoral) channels through which the group can be related to the political system; and

(d) the coöptation of established group leaders into important positions within the political system, and, if necessary, the development of such leaders.

The mobilization of a new group into politics often adversely affects the power and participatory role of other groups. These groups typically respond either by withdrawing from politics, as the landlords on Taiwan did after the land reform, by counterorganizing, by changing the scope of the political arena, or by changing the techniques and the resources used in the arena.

One clear case of the political mobilization of a new constituency, and one which illustrates many of these points, is the role of Ayub Khan among the rural middle class in Pakistan. At the time Pakistan was created Mohammad Ali Jinnah had mobilized a new constituency, the urban middle class, into politics. The organizational expression of this constituency was the Muslim League. "By organizing a political party on democratic lines, Jinnah was able to reach the apathetic Muslim middle class. In doing so he effectively by-passed the traditional leadership to which this class had hitherto responded. While Jinnah's tactics embittered and estranged the *ulema* and other traditional leaders, it won for him the following of the literate, urban, middle-class professionals of Muslim India." "Jinnah's charismatic leadership" made it possible for the League to liberate itself from control by the reactionary landlords and "reach the average, educated Muslim of urban India."[14]

Ayub Khan "was able to perform the same function for the rural middle class" that Jinnah did for the urban middle class. Prior to his coming to power, "social stratification in the villages of West Pakistan made it impossible for the rural people, other than large landlords, to exercise any political influence." Ayub Khan consciously mobilized the rural middle class for participation in the Pakistani political arena by inaugurating governmental policies for their benefit and creating a structure of "Basic Democracies" through which they could become an effective political force. He aimed his appeal at "the millions of medium and small landholders and peasant proprietors, who inhabited the East and West Pakistan countryside. He understood the process of participation in strictly arithmetical terms. Up to 1959, the country's politics had been dominated by narrow but powerful groups. The system of Basic Democracies was a device for brushing them aside and replacing them with the vast middle class of rural Pakistan." The middle-class farmers played a major role in the elections for Basic Democracies in 1959 and then enlisted the cooperation of the civil bureaucracy to secure the credit, technology, and other resources to increase substantially their agricultural output. Profiting from this expansion, the middle-class land owners significantly expanded their share of the total land ownership during the 1960s.[15] Favorable governmental policy, combined with the reconstitution through the Basic Democracies of the structures for political participation, brought a new set of participants into the Pakistani political arena.

But, as with any expansion of political participation, there was a price to be paid. Ayub's policy antagonized the traditional large landlords, although he was subsequently able to win back their support and cooperation. The growth of the rural middle class, however, also led to the dispossession from the land of the landless laborers and the smaller landowners (that is, those who owned less than 25 acres). The former moved into the large cities. The latter emigrated to nearby towns, and it was in those towns, particularly in the Punjab, that the unrest originated in the spring of 1967 that eventually spread and led to the downfall of the Ayub Khan regime in the winter of 1968-69.[16] Ayub's policies had mobilized the rural middle class to participate politically through channels provided by the regime and had also led, in due course, to the dispossession of smaller farmers from the land. The towns to which the latter migrated became the centers of the protest, rioting, and violence that led to the overthrow of the regime.

Effects on Participation of Other Elite Goals

The attitudes and actions of elites in pursuit of goals other than simple power also affect the level and nature of political participation in a society. Depending on national circumstances and elite ideology, the elites may view political participation as necessary, antithetical, or irrelevant to goals such as national independence, social welfare, economic development, national integration, or revolutionary change.

Among these goals, revolutionary change is most clearly and consistently coupled with the expansion of political participation. An elite that seeks to alter fundamentally a society's institutions, values, and social structure must dramatically expand participation, bringing new groups into politics through new, and usually disruptive or violent, forms of political activity. An essential characteristic of any major socio-political revolution is a participation explosion that sweeps aside existing elites and institutions and, if it is successful, leads to the creation of new political-social institutions that provide for both more highly centralized power and higher levels of political participation. At the local level in Vietnam, for instance, the takeover of a village by the Viet Cong normally expanded the circle of people playing critical roles in village decision-making by five to ten times. Unlike traditional village leaders, or those oriented toward the Saigon Government, the Viet Cong leaders attempted to strengthen their control over the village and to achieve their socio-economic goals by expanding participation in the village government, which they dominated.[17]

If an elite in power wishes to bring about fundamental changes in social structure and economic institutions, it will be impelled to mobilize high levels of political participation. In this situation, however, the elite may be cross-pressured. While mobilization of the masses may be necessary to social revolution, it may also contribute to political instability. Hence, elites who come to power with a commitment to fundamental change, but without a prior expansion of political participation, often follow somewhat indecisive socio-economic policies. The military government of Peru provides an excellent example of this ambivalence. On the one hand, it decreed several basic changes in social and economic policy. On the other hand, it had the typical military suspicion of widespread popular participation in public affairs. It tried to reconcile these conflicting values by devising new forms of corporate representation and participation, but the history of these efforts to date suggests that they have tended to become more means of management and control than channels of participation.[18] At best, new forms of participation at the enterprise and local level are devised, which are then isolated from the more purely "political" decision-making processes at the national level. At worst, the goals of order, effective management, and the maintenance of a clear system of hierarchy take precedence over more sweeping reforms, and, as a result, political participation is effectively downgraded.

As our discussion of alternative models has suggested, societies that have reached later stages of development must often choose whether to give priority to economic development or to socio-economic equality. Elites that prefer the technocratic model will reduce political participation drastically in order to achieve rapid growth. Those that value equality more highly will encourage higher levels of political participation to help achieve this goal. The choices on participation strategies are essentially choices of the elite, dictated by their preferences for other goals. At earlier stages of development, elites may give priority to promoting rural equality, in which case they generally disapprove of immediate efforts to broaden political participation, or they may encourage the development of an urban middle class, which usually involves a more immediate expansion of political participation.

Societies that evolve from colonial to independent status also confront their elites with a sequence of goal choices, which are clearly related to the value they put on participation. In the early stages of the nationalist movement in these societies, the leadership is often moderate and conservative, with many ties to the traditional elites. Such leaders expect to achieve independence or autonomy for their societies through a gradual process of negotiations with, and compromises by, the colonial power. By and large, they do not see the need for mobilizing mass support behind the independence movement. At some point, however, these moderate leaders are displaced by more radical nationalist leaders who seek full independence immediately and who, through a mixture of charismatic appeal and political organization, attempt to mobilize the masses of the population into the nationalist movement in order to achieve this goal. Independence is usually achieved under these leaders, and they come to power with independence. They initially attempt to maintain the high levels of participation that characterized the period immediately before and after independence. Fairly quickly, however, the levels of political involvement and activity begin to decline, in part because the cadres who played a critical role in the nationalist movement, which expanded participation, shift from the nationalist party to the governmental bureaucracy. Party organization declines and the nationalist leader often loses his mobilizing appeal as independence proves not to be a panacea for social tensions and economic problems.

At this point, the time is ripe for a shift from the radical nationalist leaders to new leaders with still different perspectives on participation. These "third generation" leaders may be one of two types. A military (or in some rare instances, a civilian) coup d'etat may bring to power a more managerially oriented technocratic regime that gives priority to financial orthodoxy and planned economic development rather than to the expansion of political participation. In fact, the achievement by these new leaders of their economic objectives often requires substantial departicipation, since the austerity measures that are involved may adversely affect important groups in the population.[19] Alternatively, in those countries that maintain democratic political systems and competitive elections, the second generation leaders may be displaced by more provincial and traditional political leaders. These new leaders often combine communal appeals (ethnic or religious) with appeals to economic self-interest in an effort to mobilize more conservative rural and provincial majorities and to oust the nationalist leaders whose support came primarily from the more modern sectors of the society. In these instances, political participation may expand, but the bases upon which it is organized may shift toward more traditional patterns.

Administration of Governmental Programs

The impact of elite choices on political participation goes beyond the elites' strategies for gaining and holding power and their choice of national priorities. More mundane decisions regarding the organization and administration of government programs can also significantly affect the nature and pattern of participation in a society. Sometimes programs are deliberately designed to expand or contract political participation, in line with broader strategic decisions about the value of participation as a means toward other goals. Sometimes choices of organizational and administrative techniques are made on entirely different grounds, and the effects on participation are unanticipated by-products.

In all developing nations, the scope of government activity expands as modernization proceeds. The general effects that increasingly pervasive government programs have on political participation (and vice versa) are discussed in Chapter Three. Here we are less concerned with the fact of expanding programs than we are with elite choices concerning how the programs are administered, and with how this administration may, in turn, affect participation.

One administrative choice that confronts elites is the extent to which the government should assume direct responsibility for implementing specific programs or should urge citizens themselves to take on more responsibility. For example, national leaders can encourage villages or urban neighborhoods which need new facilities or services either to act on their own to meet their needs or to look to the government for help. In a comparison of preferred responses among urban migrants in Mexico City and Lima, for instance, it has been shown that migrants in the latter city relied considerably more on self-help, while those in Mexico City were more likely to turn to the government. These different responses are explained as a result of the choices made by governmental elites about policies and programs. "In the case of Peru, most governments since the late 1950s have sought to stimulate and capitalize upon the self-help efforts of low-income city dwellers." As a result, "large and effective self-help projects were launched in many of the squatter settlements ringing large cities." In Mexico, on the other hand, the reluctance of both urban and rural low-income citizens to resort to self-help "reflects the efforts of successive governments since 1940 to encourage a sense of mass dependence upon the regime for community improvements and other types of social benefits." In countries like Chile and Venezuela that have had competitive party systems, political elites have also felt the need to be responsive to the needs of low-income communities and hence the "residents of such communities have devoted most of their energies to petitioning activities rather than to self-help efforts." Thus, the extent to which low-income urban residents resort to self-help or to political action is a function of both the competitiveness of the party system and "the presence or absence of overt governmental attempts to create feelings of dependence among the lower classes."[20]

In Kenya, as in Peru, the government also encouraged local self-help projects, as exemplified particularly in the building of the community-built secondary or "Harambee" schools. It consciously "preferred local participation through concrete self-help projects to participation in competitive politics expressed electorally." Once the idea got started, however, each community wanted to have its own school. The spread of self-help projects led to the central government attempting to control their proliferation because they would generate claims for state aid. "The present regime, after first fostering local participation around the building of Harambee schools is now nervous about the consequences for its budget."[21] Thus, while self-help may initially be conceived by the government as a way of deflecting demands and pressures and, in effect, of depoliticizing issues, the spread of self-help projects may eventually lead to new, unplanned, and more diversified claims for governmental assistance. By stimulating dependence on government, political leaders encourage direct contacting by individuals or communities when particular needs arise. By stimulating a self-help ethos, political leaders encourage the development of community organizations, which may then be in a position to make broader and more effective demands on government. In the context of development, even activity that is purposefully designed to be non-political cannot, apparently, remain isolated from politics for very long.

Even where self-help is not involved, the particular forms of administration chosen for government programs may affect political participation. Land reform, for instance, can be carried out by a single centralized governmental bureaucracy, can be decentralized to a number of new and old governmental agencies, or can be devolved to local governmental bodies. A study of land reform in twenty-five countries found that in only one out of nine cases of centralized administration, and in none of six cases of decentralized administration, was the land reform accompanied by a significant increase in the political power of peasants, either through an improvement in their status as land owners or through an increased ability to influence local governmental decisions. In eight out of ten cases where land reform functions were devolved to local governmental bodies, on the other hand, the political power of the former tenants increased significantly.[22] Thus, a program designed primarily to achieve another goal, the promotion of socio-economic equality, can be administered so as to promote, or not, the expansion of political participation. In developing countries, in general, political elites can choose to administer programs with a broad impact upon substantial portions of the population through either participation-enhancing, participation-neutral, or participation-reducing ways.

Participation in Development: Goal, Means, or By-Product?

In the overall process of development, the expansion of political participation can conceivably be: (a) a primary goal of the political elites, social forces, and individuals involved in the process; (b) a means by which elites, groups, and individuals achieve other goals that they value highly; or (c) a by-product or consequence of the achievement of other goals, either by societies as a whole, or by elites, groups, and individuals within those societies. Or, and we do not mean to be facetious, it could also quite conceivably be none of the above.

As we have suggested, the expansion of political participation is seldom a primary goal for political elites in a developing society. The extent to which political participation does expand reflects in large part the extent to which it is either a means to the achievement of other goals or a by-product of that achievement. Political leaders will attempt to expand political participation if they see the expansion as a way of promoting or maintaining their power and of fostering other goals they think desirable, such as national independence or socio-economic equality. Those with political power, and hence with the capability of affecting political participation, are, however, more likely to attempt to bolster their own power and promote political stability by restricting political participation than by expanding it. On the other hand, the pursuit of goals such as economic development, socio-economic equality, and even political stability, can generate conditions conducive to the expansion of political participation. Similarly, the ways in which political and governmental elites choose to implement governmental programs have important consequences for the extent and character of political participation.

Groups and individuals within a developing society are also unlikely to value political participation as a goal in itself, and are more likely to resort first to other possible ways of improving their social status and material well-being. The achievement of these other goals, however, may well increase political participation. In general, then, political participation is not likely to be pursued as a goal in itself; it may, at times, be pursued on an instrumental basis as a means to the achievement of another goal; and it is most likely to appear as the by-product of achieving some other goal.

3

Development, Equality, and Participation

The Relations among These Variables

The achievement of two goals in particular has been linked, in social science literature and in the liberal model of development, with the consequent expansion of political participation. The *development* hypothesis holds that higher levels of socio-economic development in a society lead to higher levels of political participation and, implicitly, to a shift from mobilized to autonomous participation. The *equality* hypothesis holds that higher levels of socio-economic equality lead to higher levels of political participation. Conceivably, one or the other of these hypotheses could be true, both could be true, both could be false, or one could be true under some circumstances and the other true under different circumstances. This issue is, obviously, of crucial importance to both analysts and practitioners of development. If one's goal is to promote political participation, should one be more favorably disposed towards political elites that give higher priority to socio-economic development and economic growth, or towards elites that put greater emphasis on the achievement of social and economic equality?

As we have pointed out, the liberal model of development assumes both hypotheses to be true, and also assumes a positive relation between development and equality. Our review of the evidence suggests that, in all phases of development, higher levels both of socio-economic development and of socio-economic equality do indeed lead to higher levels of political participation. But the reverse is not always true; in the earlier phases of development, higher levels of political participation promote lower levels of socio-economic equality (bourgeois vs. autocratic models), while in the later phases of development, higher levels of

42

political participation tend to produce lower rates of economic growth (populist vs. technocratic models).

The Impact of Development on Levels of Participation

"Traditional society," declared Daniel Lerner in 1958, "is non-participant . . . Modern society is participant . . . . ."[1] In the years since, it has become commonly accepted that the principal political difference between traditional and modern societies is the scope, intensity, and bases of political participation. In more wealthy, industrialized, ur-banized, complex societies, more people become involved in politics in more ways than they do in less developed, agricultural, rural, more primitive economic and social systems. "It comes as no surprise," commented one set of authors a decade after Lerner, "to learn that a nation's level of political participation co-varies with its level of economic development."[2] The cross-national and longitudinal evidence to support this proposition is overwhelming, ranging from apparently global relationships between the level of political mobilization and the distribution of employment among the primary, secondary, and tertiary sectors on the one hand, to the discovery that levels of voting participation among the fifty states "are a function of levels of economic development."[3] Socio-economic modernity and political participation seem to march hand-in-hand through history. The higher the level of socio-economic development in a society, the higher the level of political participation.

Why Development Promotes Participation

Why should there be this relationship between socio-economic de-velopment and political participation? At a broad level, several links are apparent.

First, within a society, levels of political participation tend to vary with socio-economic status. Those with more education, more income, and higher-status occupations usually participate more than those who are poor, uneducated, and in low-status occupations. Economic devel-opment expands the proportion of higher status roles in a society: more people become literate, educated, prosperous, and work in middle-class occupations. Hence a larger proportion of society becomes politically participant.

Second, economic and social development involves tensions and strains among social groups: new groups emerge, established groups are threatened, and low-status groups seize opportunities to improve their lot. As a result, conflicts multiply between social classes, regions, and communal groups. Social conflict intensifies and in some cases virtually creates group consciousness, which in turn leads to collective action by a group to develop and protect its claims vis-a-vis other groups. It must, in short, turn to politics.

Third, the growing complexity of the economy leads to a multiplying of organizations and associations and to the involvement of larger numbers of people in such groups. Business organizations, farmer associations, labor unions, community organizations, as well as cultural, recreational, and even religious organizations, are more characteristic of more highly developed societies. In Turkey, for instance, economic development has been accompanied by a marked increase in the number of associations and the "population/association ratio is noticeably higher in the less developed provinces than in the more developed ones. Both findings suggest a positive relationship between socio-economic development and the intensity of associational activity."[4] Organizational involvement is also generally associated with political participation.

Fourth, economic development partly requires and partly produces a notable expansion of the functions of government. While the scope of governmental activity is clearly influenced by the political values and ideologies dominant in the society, it is even more clearly influenced by the level of economic development in the society. Highly industrialized societies that are run by governments devoted to free-enterprise capitalism often have more highly socialized economies than agrarian societies run by committed socialists. The former simply require more governmental promotion, regulation, and redistribution. The more the government's actions affect groups within society, however, the more those groups will see the relevance of government to their own ends, and the more active they will become in their efforts to influence governmental decision-making.

Fifth, socio-economic modernization normally takes place in the form of national development. The nation-state is the vehicle of socio-economic modernization. For the individual, consequently, his relationship with the nation-state becomes critical, and his identity as a part of the state tends to override his other loyalties. That identity is theoretically expressed in the concept of citizenship, which presumably overrides distinctions of social class and communal group, and which furnishes the basis for mass political participation. All citizens are equal before the state; all have certain minimal equal rights and responsbilities as participants in the state. Socio-economic modernization thus implies a political culture and outlook that in some measure legitimizes, and hence facilitates, political participation. And this is the case in both democratic and communist societies.

When Development Does Not Promote Participation

Given the pronouncements of social scientists, the weight of the statistical evidence, and these seemingly persuasive causal relationships, one might well expect a more or less one-to-one relationship between the level of socio-economic development in a society and the level of political participation.

In fact, however, this is far from the case. While there is a general tendency for many forms of national political participation to increase with economic development, this is by no means a universal phenomenon. Other things being equal, economic development tends to enhance political participation. But other things are rarely equal, and there are many factors, not necessarily shaped by economic development, that in themselves shape political participation. Since we cannot meaningfully sum the different forms of political participation, it is extremely difficult to judge the overall level of political participation in a society. Particular forms of participation, however, may vary independently of socio-economic development.

Socio-economic development normally increases more or less steadily with time. In many societies, however, levels of voting or other forms of political participation fluctuate quite widely over brief periods of time. There may be sudden expansions ("participation explosions") and equally well marked declines in participation. "[I]n many countries that are still considered relatively underdeveloped," Brunner and Brewer have observed, "there are already very high levels of voting turnout, and there seems to be no clear secular trend toward increasing levels of turnout."[5] In Turkey and Colombia in the years after World War II there were periods when voting participation substantially decreased. Such figures may mean that voting rates do not reflect overall participation levels. Conceivably, an underdeveloped country could have high levels of voting participation but low levels of other forms of participation. Conceivably, too, as the country developed further, voting rates could decline, as other types of participation became more widespread. At least some evidence suggests, however, that the decline may not be limited to voting. In Kenya, Uganda, and other African states, political participation levels apparently peaked in the years immediately before and after independence and were then followed by significant departicipation.[6] Certainly the prevalent forms of participation change from time to time. In Kenya, for instance, an "independence style cluster" of political participation, emphasizing electoral activity, rallies, party membership, and dues paying, was supplanted by a "post-independence style cluster," characterized by the acquisition of information about government and the presentation of views and demands to governmental decision-makers.[7] Similarly, the participation levels of particular groups in the society may vary over time, with apparently little relation to levels of socio-economic modernization. Such changes at both the group and the society level may be sustained long enough that they cannot be written off simply as temporary aberrations from the socio-economic development model.

Not only do levels of participation within societies often fluctuate sharply and independently of trends in socio-economic development, but differences in levels of political participation among societies do not necessarily correspond with differences in their levels of socio-economic development. The poor communist societies in Asia (particularly China and North Vietnam) clearly have had extraordinarily high levels of mobilized participation. Many societies that are much less economically developed than the United States have substantially higher rates of voting participation. Within societies also, differences in participation rates do not necessarily correspond with differences in socio-economic modernization. In Turkey, India, and elsewhere, voting participation is often higher in the less developed parts of the country than in the more developed parts. Even in the United States, where there is a strong correlation between voting turnout and economic development among the states, a state like West Virginia may deviate significantly from this pattern and have a high level of turnout despite a relatively low level of economic development.

More generally, some aspects of modernization appear to have little direct relationship with political participation. It has, for instance, often been assumed that urbanization promotes political participation. In his pioneering work in the late 1950s, Lerner, indeed, assigned a primary role to urbanization. He hypothesized, and his data seemed to support, the proposition that urbanization led to literacy, which led to media consumption, which, in turn, was related to political participation. Other scholars subsequently analyzed these presumed causal relationships and came up with somewhat different patterns, although they still attributed a major primary role to urbanization. In fact, however, there does not appear to be any consistent global difference in the levels of rural and urban political participation. Many countries show no real differences between urban and rural participation rates; in some countries, such as France, Turkey, Japan, the Philippines, and Pakistan, rural voting rates have been higher than urban ones.[8] In some countries, such as Chile, the levels of urban and rural voting rates have changed significantly over time, with a relative decrease in the latter and an increase in the former.[9]

In those countries where urban participation rates are higher, the apparent direct relationship is spurious, a result of differences in education and occupation. When these factors are held constant, locality size and length of urban residence appear to have no significant independent effect on political participation. In his comparative analysis of the factors responsible for "active citizenship" among working-class men in six countries, Inkeles found a mild relationship between length of urban residence and active citizenship in Argentina, Chile, and Nigeria, but a much weaker relationship in India and East Pakistan. Once education and factory experience were controlled for, however, these relationships disappeared and, indeed, in Argentina and Chile the effect of urbanization became mildly negative.[10] Urbanism thus had no independent effect on active citizenship. In another study of India, it was found that when education was controlled, "those who live in the cities vote *slightly* less frequently than those who live in the rural areas."[11] In their re-analysis of the Almond-Verba data for the United States, United Kingdom, Germany, Italy, and Mexico, Nie and his associates came to a similar conclusion. Urbanization, in terms of the size of the place of residence, had no independent impact on overall political participation and in only one marginal instance (the United States) on national political participation. On the other hand, there were consistent weak negative correlations between size of locality and efforts to influence local governmental decisions. In no instance, however, did urbanization explain more than two percent of the variance in participation.[12] In short, where urban political participation is higher than rural participation, it is the result of differences in social status, education, and occupation. In terms of aggregate voting rates, much of the difference between urban and rural residence has been due to the differences between the voting rates of women. Over time, historically in Europe and more recently in India, the differences between rural and urban voting turnout tend to decline as the voting rates of rural women begin to approximate those of urban women.[13]

Why Development Does Not Always Promote Participation

What produces these variations from the otherwise prevailing relationship between development and participation? The explanations are to be found in the extent to which the factors that increase the levels of political participation are produced by causes other than socio-economic development and in the extent to which socio-economic development produces factors that have a negative, as well as positive, effect on levels of political participation.

First, many of the factors that are related to socio-economic development, or are affected by it, and which in turn promote political participation, may themselves have causes other than the process of socio-economic development itself. The one factor promoting political participation that appears unlikely to vary independently of socio-economic development is the status structure in society. As societies become more developed, however, variations in political participation may be shaped less by status structure and more by political and organizational factors, which are not necessarily determined by the level of economic development. On the other hand, group conflict and consciousness, organizational involvement, and the expansion of governmental activities, all of which tend to be promoted by the processes of economic development, may also result from other causes. Migration, exploitation, war, aggression, political leadership, and ideological and religious differences can all, quite independently of economic development, promote more group consciousness, organizational involvement, and governmental activity, which, in turn, are likely to promote more political participation. Thus, in Hispanic America in the late eighteenth and early nineteenth centuries, levels of political participation were achieved that could not be explained by socio-economic development or socio-economic equality, but were, instead, the result of group interaction, migration, and war.[14] Foreign and civil war, indeed, may well rank a close second to socio-economic development in the ability to stimulate the emergence of national consciousness, the expansion of governmental activity, higher levels of social mobilization, and more organizational involvement and group interaction. Through these intermediate variables war has an impact on levels of political participation that is particularly noticeable when previously nonparticipant or marginally-participant groups are mobilized to fight on behalf of a society or nation that previously excluded them from many of the most important attributes of membership. Cases cited to support this proposition range from the impact of World War II on the American Negro to the impact of the Chaco War on the Bolivian peasant. Also, at times of dislocation in a society, ideological or religious appeals may become particularly potent in mobilizing groups for political and military action.

Second, there are also some ways in which socio-economic development may tend to reduce political participation. The expansion of the scope of governmental activity, for instance, may have negative as well as positive consequences for the levels of political participation. People are likely to perceive government as more relevant to their own concerns, but this need not be accompanied by feelings of an increased ability to influence government. The increasing concentration of governmental activities at the national level, and away from the local level, may well have just the reverse effect. So also may the increased specialization in governmental activities, the professionalization of governmental personnel, and the increased proportion of complex and technical programs and policies. In traditional society, governmental decisions are more likely to deal with individual benefits or particularistic issues. Socio-economic modernization is likely to promote a relative decline of particularistic decision-making, a marked expansion of more generalized decision-making dealing with collective benefits, and the development of more routinized procedures for handling individual needs. The opportunities for personal contacting and small-group lobbying, particularly by low-status individuals and groups, may consequently be reduced. Modernization may also increase the social distance between governmental officials and low-status citizens. The peasant who could appeal to, and even negotiate with, the village chief or local landlord may be totally incapable of dealing with the urban-trained agrarian reform official sent out from the capital city. Özbudun, for instance, found the most widespread feelings of political efficacy in the two least developed regions of Turkey. This, he suggests, "can be attributed either to the greater ease of contacting the locally elected officials (village headman and the Council of Elders) in the smaller and more tightly-knit village communities of Eastern regions, or to a lack of political realism usually associated with low levels of objective and attitudinal modernization."[15]

The purpose of political participation is to affect governmental decision-making. Consequently, such activity has to be directed at, and have an impact on, the loci where decisions are made. In a traditional society, most decisions affecting villagers' lives are presumably made by the village chiefs and council, who are therefore the targets of whatever political participation the villagers engage in. As society becomes more modern, however, an increasing proportion of the governmental decision-making that affects the villagers takes place, not at the village level, but at the national level. This shift in the locus of decision-making is likely to occur much more rapidly than the shift in the locus of political action by the villagers. Thus, in a traditional society, perhaps ninety percent of the governmental decisions affecting a villager are made at the village level and ten percent at the national level. As the society modernizes, the distribution may rapidly approach fifty-fifty. In all likelihood, however, the bulk of the political participation of the villager, say eighty percent, is still focused at the village level. The amount of national governmental decision-making that affects the society increases at a faster rate than the amount of political participation affecting national government. Thus, the ratio of political activity by individuals to the governmental decisions affecting them actually goes down. In addition, of course, the inhabitants of any one village can expect to have only marginal influence on decisions that affect many villages. Hence, while the total amount of political participation may increase in society, so also may the feelings of alienation and political inefficacy.

Socio-economic development also tends to increase the functional specificity of relationships and organizations, including those related to politics. In a traditional agrarian society, the elite and mass are presumably related to each other through diffuse ties, encompassing economic, social, religious, and political relationships. This multifunctionality of relationships makes it easier for the landlord or village chief to mobilize his followers for political purposes. In Turkey, India, and elsewhere, the highest voting turnouts are precisely in those traditional rural areas where the local leaders can capitalize on their social prestige, cultural superiority, economic incentives, and implied or explicit coercion to mobilize their supporters to the polls. In a modern society, political organizers attempt to create "parties of integration" designed to provide comparable diffuse multifunctional relationships and high levels of political participation. Such parties combine social, cultural, and welfare functions with purely political ones, and also tend to be very successful in producing substantial turnouts for rallies, campaign work, and other activities. Purely political organizations and leaders, in contrast, are not likely to produce comparable rates of participation. Organizational multifunctionality, in short, correlates positively with political participation. The overall tendency in modernizing societies, however, is toward more specific functional relationships. To the extent that this occurs in politics, that is, to the extent that organs of political participation become distinct and specialize purely in political participation, they will become less successful at it. The expansion of political participation leads, paradoxically, to the development of a professional political class, which, by segregating political relationships from other relationships, tends to reduce or to limit political participation.

Economic development also tends to multiply the opportunities for individual social and economic mobility, both horizontal and vertical. In the short run, individual social mobility is likely to decrease political participation. For most people, political participation is simply a means to other goals. If individuals can achieve these goals by moving to the city, by shifting to higher-status employment, or by improving their economic well-being, these are, in some measure, substitutes for political participation. More generally, in Hirschman's terms, the multiplication of the opportunities for and incentives to "exit" reduces the probability that people will resort to "voice."[16] Confronted with increasing economic uncertainty and a declining standard of living, a peasant is more likely to move to the city than to engage in corrective political action, provided the costs of migration are bearable. (See Chapter Four.) Economic development—communications networks, roads, buslines, urban job opportunities—reduces the uncertainties and costs of migration and thus lowers the level of rural political participation. Where migration is impossible or difficult, other things being equal, peasants are more likely to resort to politics, despite its uncertainties and risks. In a similar fashion, when confronted with a neighborhood problem in a central city, whites, who have a choice between migration and political action, are likely to choose the former, while blacks, for whom migration is presumably a much less realistic option, are more likely to resort to politics.[17]

The fact that urban political participation rates are not higher than rural rates, once education and occupation are controlled for, suggests that there may be compensating features in the urban environment that keep participation down, despite the presumably more intense stimuli from mass media and interpersonal contacts. The broader opportunities for social and economic mobility—to achieve higher levels of education and occupational status—will increase political participation in the long run, but may, in the short run, tend to reduce it. Economic development may produce greater pressures and stimuli to participate in politics but it may also lessen the incentive to do so by opening up more appealing opportunities to participate in other things.

Reformulating the Development-Participation Relationship

On balance, socio-economic development creates conditions favoring higher levels of political participation. But socio-economic development can also at times tend to moderate participation levels. The consequences of socio-economic modernization for political participation are not necessarily uniform from one society to another. What determines whether socio-economic modernization is likely to have a highly positive or a more ambivalent effect on political participation? One critical factor, obviously, is the attitude of the political elite towards political participation. (See Chapter Two.) Another major factor may be the degree of group consciousness and cohesiveness that exists in a traditional society entering into socio-economic modernization. In societies that are "group weak," that is, societies in which overall group consciousness and organizational involvement are relatively low, socio-economic modernization may well reduce political participation. In such societies, political organizations are more likely to be functionally specific, and mobility or exit options are more likely to appeal to individuals. The isolated individual, not well integrated into a group or "little platoon," is likely to feel more overwhelmed and less efficacious when confronted by the growing role of the national government. On the other hand, in a society that is "group strong," in which there is a tradition of family, ethnic, religious, or territorial groupings and associations, the process of socio-economic modernization is likely to reinforce these identifications and to enhance the ability and motivation of individuals to mobilize and organize for political action on the basis of preexisting or primordial ties.

Thus, the development hypothesis that posits a fairly straight-forward linear relationship between levels of socio-economic development and levels of political participation needs to be modified in two ways. In general, development and participation do go hand-in-hand, but in some cases some participation can occur without development, and in others some development can occur without participation. In particular, the involvement of a society in a major and traumatic war may produce significant increases in its levels of political participation without the normally corresponding changes in its overall level of socio-economic development. Conversely, in a society where traditional group cohesion and consciousness is low, socio-economic development may have an ambivalent effect on the levels of political participation. Thus, with respect to the promotion of political participation, the impact of a society's external environment may compensate, in part, for a lower level of socio-economic development, and the impact of its traditional culture and behavior patterns may counterbalance, in part, the effects of higher levels of socio-economic development.

The Impact of Development on Patterns of Participation

Changes in the level of socio-economic development affect the nature as well as the levels of political participation. In the most backward societies there is little mobilized or autonomous participation, particularly outside local politics. As socio-economic change takes place, however, first mobilized, and eventually autonomous, participation begins to expand. The high levels of voting participation reported in rural, as compared to urban, areas of countries such as India, Turkey, Pakistan, and the Philippines are produced in large part by landlords mobilizing voters to the polls through patron-client ties.[18] In Turkey, voting rates are higher in the less developed villages and regions, and at the individual level voting is not significantly related to political information, national identification, desire for political participation, or any other attitudinal aspects of participation except feelings of political efficacy. The latter feelings, however, are usually with respect to local rather than national authorities. It seems reasonable to conclude that there is "a considerable amount of mobilized participation among Turkish peasants, especially in the less developed villages. In such villages, traditional notables (wealthy landlords, tribal chiefs, or religious leaders) are usually able to secure high turnout rates and high voting percentages for the parties they support."[19] The introduction of competitive elections into a traditional society thus provides a tremendous stimulus for mobilized voting participation.

In societies in the early and intermediate levels of development, mobilized participation may also expand through other means and in urban as well as rural areas. In the absence of competitive elections, a strong single party may produce, at least for brief periods of time, substantial levels of mobilized political activity. In the cities, labor union leaders and local political bosses may be able to accomplish similar results. In due course, however, socio-economic development changes the distribution of statuses within a society and increases the importance of autonomous, as compared to mobilized, participation. In general, the level of mobilized participation in a society probably has an inverted U-shaped relation and the level of autonomous participation a linear relation to the level of socio-economic development.

The changing importance of autonomous and mobilized participation may also be reflected in the changing importance of different forms of participation. In an area like the Turkish countryside, where voting is largely a function of mobilization, voting rates may remain high and stable, despite changes in the national political scene. "In the urban centers," on the other hand, "voting is largely an autonomous act, a matter of individual decision," and "some voters may simply lack the motivation to vote." There is every reason to believe that urban residents are at least as well "politically informed, concerned, interested, and involved" as the villagers, and associational and other collective activity related to politics is clearly more widespread in the cities than in the countryside.[20] The decline in mobilized participation in the cities is reflected in a decline in voting rates; the rise of autonomous participation is reflected in higher levels of other forms of political activity.

As societies modernize, the bases of political participation also change. A simple theory of political modernization would suggest a clear displacement of more traditional bases (patron-client and communal group) by more modern ones (class and party). As with participation levels, however, there is no one-to-one relation between these changes and socio-economic development. Instead, development is more likely to supplement the traditional bases with other bases. In a more modern society, the bases of participation will be more complex and diverse than in a traditional society. The relationship between the principal bases of political participation, and the levels of development and sectors of a society can be represented more or less as follows:

Level of Development of Society	Sector	
	Rural	Urban
Low	Patron-client	Elite faction
Medium	Patron-client or Class	Patron-client (*cacique*) Machine Neighborhood Communal group
High	Class/party	Class/party Neighborhood Communal group/party

In traditional societies, *patron-client relations* provide a means for the vertical mobilization of lower-status individuals by established elites. In purely traditional societies, patron-client relations may exist without any political dimension. The introduction of competitive elections gives the client one additional resource—the vote—which he can use to repay his patron for other benefits. In the 1960s, patron-client relationships remained a continuingly important feature of politics in India, the Philippines, Turkey, and Colombia. In these countries, patron-client groups often formed the basic local unit of party politics, with one leading local figure lining up with one party and mobilizing his followers for that party, while rival local leaders worked through other parties. "Economic competition among the landholding elites in rural communities," Powell observes, "is what provides the motive for political competition, or factionalism." This pattern of factionalism "does not seem to be confined to the most backward and traditional communities, but may persist for some time under the impact of economic modernization if intra-elite local competition revolves around a limited number of activities."[21]

Eventually, however, the commercialization of agriculture and the socio-economic development of the countryside undermine the rural basis for patron-client politics. In a rural area, unlike a city, it may be difficult for different bases of political participation to coexist side-by-side. In some instances, patron-client ties may prevail in local politics and class-based behavior in national politics. But "as economic modernization further proceeds, drawing local elites into what may be specialized roles which complement, rather than compete or conflict with one another, then local electoral patterns may shift away from elite mobilization of peasant dependents toward a class-conflict pattern." This will be more markedly the case if traditional landowners are supplanted by new, capitalistic owners who cease to perform the social, ceremonial, and welfare functions that traditionally would be theirs in the patron-client relationship.[22]

In a more traditional society, the patron might be associated with a national political party, but he could also change his party allegiance and, with his secure local rural base, he could often afford to be relatively independent of party. The impact of external economic forces on the countryside compels the development of a more formalized political organization, which can promote and defend the economic interests of the principal groups in the region in the conflicts of national politics. If there are substantial numbers of subsistence farmers and small-scale capitalist farmers, plus perhaps some latifundia, this political participation is likely to take the form of an agrarian populist party that cuts across economic class lines and unites these rural groups in terms of their common interests vis-a-vis urban society. If, on the other hand, there are large-scale capitalist farms or nonpaternalistic latifundia with substantial numbers of sub-subsistence peasants and landless laborers, the latter are more likely to be mobilized into radical leftist parties. This is particularly likely to happen if the class polarization coincides with an ethnic cleavage between owners and nonowners.[23]

In the absence of conscious and assiduously administered government policies designed to promote greater equality in income and land ownership, the processes of economic modernization in the countryside normally tend to strengthen existing inequalities and hence to increase the likelihood of class-based politics. New owners, new capital investment, and new technology all generally accelerate this process. In those areas of India and Pakistan, for instance, that were exposed most extensively to the "green revolution,"

> traditional hierarchical arrangements rooted in norms of mutual interdependence and (non-symmetric) obligations give way to adversary relations between large landowners and the landless based on new notions of economic interest. Multi-caste/class political factions led by traditional landowning patrons and constructed with the support of low status landless groups are more difficult to sustain as viable political units. Instead, in areas most affected by the green revolution effective political mobilization depends increasingly on direct appeals to the aspirations of the poor peasantry.[24]

Migration of peasants to the cities removes potential clients from the rural patron-client system. It may also, however, reinforce the stability of that system in the countryside by draining off surplus population, which might otherwise lead to class and revolutionary politics. Cityward migration also can lead to the introduction of patron-client patterns into the urban environment. This is especially likely to occur when rural elites also move into the city, as has happened in some Brazilian cities. Beyond that, the relations between the urban migrant and urban *cacique,* or ward boss, often resemble those of the rural patron-client. There are, however, two differences: (1) the urban *cacique*-client relationship is more explicitly and primarily political in character; (2) there is likely to be less difference in status between *cacique* and client in the city.

In the urban areas, patron-client relations gradually tend to lose their predominantly personal character and to evolve into more institutionalized machine politics. Even in societies at high levels of development, however, the underlying cliental patterns may remain. The Liberal Democratic Party in Japan, for instance, maintained its voting strength, despite the migration of its rural constituents into the cities, by developing local associations (*koenkai*) around individual leaders; these associations essentially involve complex patron-client exchanges. Some of the associations have 20,000 to 30,000 members and the entire system is appropriately called one of "organizational clientelism."[25]

In cities where a substantial portion of the urban migrants are only temporary urban residents, as in Africa, political organization is often based on the rural-rooted ties of tribe and village of origin. In other countries, such as Korea, where cultural traditions and political restraints are unfavorable, even permanent urban migrants may find little basis for organization in terms of either rural origins or urban residence. In Latin America, Turkey, and the Philippines, on the other hand, the *neighborhood* is an important base of political organization for low-income urbanites. This is particularly true in new settlements. Many of the most important services that city government provides are distributed on a geographical basis: water supply, sewage disposal, and police and fire protection. Neighborhoods organize to demand these services. New settlements may also have to establish their collective or individual rights to land and to legal recognition. In rural areas, the village may be a base for political organization, but, except in some circumstances, the competition among villages is less intense than that among urban barrios.

In the initial organization of Latin American low-income neighborhoods, a critical role may be played, at times, by a personalistic local leader or *cacique*. "The emergence of *caciquismo* as a pattern of local level leadership in such areas," Cornelius has observed, is likely to "be related both to the illegality of their origins and the magnitude of the developmental needs and problems which they confront." It may also, as has often been argued, be the result of the "residual ruralism" of the urban migrants, that is, the "transference of leadership role expectations from life in the rural community to that of the urban squatter settlements." The waning of these attitudes, the diversification of the squatter community, governmental recognition of the claims of the community to land and legality, and the development of more complex and diverse relationships between the community and the urban society at large, all tend to weaken the role of the *cacique* and the patron-client relationships upon which his power depends. Hence it is probably accurate "to conceive of urban *caciquismo* as a transitory phenomenon restricted to a particular phase in the evolution of a low-income settlement zone and the urban assimilation of its population." With the passing of the *cacique,* his place is likely to be taken by governmental agencies, by more formalized party structures, and by occupational or class-based associations.[26]

In general, *party-based participation* increases with socio-economic development. In some instances, as with the Leninist party of professional revolutionaries, the political party may be a primary base of political identification and action. More frequently, the party is a supplementary overlay that serves as a vehicle of political expression for some other type of group, or serves as a way of coordinating and integrating the political activities of two or more groups. Other bases of political organization typically reflect more specialized motives and interests on the part of their members. The party differs in that it often attempts to unite mobilized and autonomous participants, for particular political objectives, and it may, in some measure, combine a variety of other different bases of participation. Parties tend to be stronger and to play a more important role in fostering political participation if they are tied closely to traditional patron-client groupings, communal groups, or occupation-class groups such as peasant syndicates and labor unions. The level of participation and, to some extent, its forms will be set by the extent to which the cleavages between two or more bases of participation coincide and thus appeals to one base are reinforced by appeals to other bases.

Socio-economic development more often stimulates than reduces *communal group* consciousness, political activity, and inter-group violence. Urbanization in particular increases the likelihood of communal-based politics by intensifying relations among groups. These relations, in turn, reflect the number, size, location, and power of the groups. Different patterns of communal participation are shaped by the extent to which:

(1) There is a large number of small communal groups in the society or a small number of larger ones;

No Easy Choice

(2) Different groups have different sources of power (education, wealth, coercion, external affiliations, organization);

(3) The government is controlled by a majority, plurality, or minority communal group;

(4) Communal groups are geographically segregated in different regions or between rural and urban areas or are intermixed in close proximity;

(5) Some groups that have been viewed as backward or traditional improve their socio-economic status and threaten to produce a status reversal vis-a-vis traditionally dominant groups.

The structuring of politics on communal bases and the mobilization of people through communal appeals tend to produce higher levels of political participation than the structuring of politics in terms of patron-client relations, class, or neighborhood. It can also, of course, lead to a breakdown of cooperative relations among communal groups, increased communal hostility and antagonism, communal violence, and potentially serious threats to national integration. Hence, governments may attempt to reduce both political participation and communal group hostility because of the close relationship between the two.

It is commonly assumed that socio-economic development leads to an increase in *class-based political participation*. To the extent that development increases participation generally, the bulk of that increase is among people of lower socio-economic status; that is, each marginal increment in the number of political participants presumably has a lower average socio-economic status than the previous increment. Hence the diversity of socio-economic class among participants increases with the expansion of political participation. In itself, of course, this diversity is simply a necessary but not sufficient condition for class-based participation. People also have to be mobilized on a class basis, or they have to identify themselves autonomously with a class and consciously choose to participate in politics on the basis of that identification. It has been abundantly demonstrated that in most developed countries without sharp communal cleavages voting participation is very largely class-based. The emergence of class-based voting patterns is also evident in the historical evolution of western European societies.

In the Harvard Project, the studies of Turkey and Colombia showed signs of class-based voting in the late 1960s and early 1970s in the urban areas of both countries. In Colombia, the two traditionally dominant parties, the Liberals and the Conservatives, historically had been multi-class parties held together by patron-client networks and by intense antipathy for each other, which generated fierce partisan loyalties and gave rise, in the early 1950s, to *La Violencia,* in which thousands of people were killed in interparty strife. In the late 1950s, the two parties formed the National Front and agreed to divide the principal elected offices between them and to alternate the presidency. The result was a significant decrease in voting levels. (See Chapter Two.) In the 1970 presidential elections the National Front faced serious opposition for the first time, in the form of the candidacy of the former dictator Rojas Pinilla, head of the *Alianza Nacional Popular* (ANAPO). The election was extraordinarily close, and in sharp contrast to earlier elections, the "1970 Presidential election was marked by a very high degree of socio-economic class voting in the major cities."[27] In upper class urban barrios, Pastrana, the "official" National Front coalition candidate, got about seventy-five percent of the vote and Rojas, the opposition ANAPO candidate, less than ten percent. In lower class urban barrios, Pastrana's vote was about twenty-five percent and Rojas' vote about sixty-five percent of the total. (See Table 3.1.) This pattern of voting was directly the result of the Rojas candidacy, which made a populist appeal to the urban poor and working class voters and which also threatened middle and upper-class voters.

This pattern of sharply polarized urban class voting was not maintained, however. In the 1974 presidential elections, the National Front was dissolved, and both the Liberal and the Conservative parties ran well-known candidates, while Rojas Pinilla's daughter was the ANAPO nominee. With a renewed choice between the traditional parties (and the possible reluctance of Colombians to vote for a woman for president), the older cleavage pattern reasserted itself. ANAPO received less than ten percent of the vote. Both the Liberal and Conservative candidates were able to appeal across class lines, although the former made the most explicit efforts to win over the ANAPO voters. The class-cleavage pattern of 1970 can thus be viewed either as a temporary deviation from the continuing traditional cleavage pattern or as a foretaste of what the future holds for Colombian politics. Whether vertical cleavages will be superseded by horizontal ones would appear to

Table 3.1. Class Voting in Urban Areas, Colombia, Presidential Election, April 19, 1970

Socio-economic level of barrio	Approximate income level Pesos/month	% of total vote	% voting for			
			Pastrana	Rojas	Betancur	Other
I. Bogotá: Voting in 84 Selected Polls (of 117 Total Polls)						
Upper	Over 10,000	6.9	75.8	8.3	11.3	3.9
Upper-middle	5,001-10,000	7.3	67.0	11.9	17.6	3.0
Middle	2,001-5,000	19.5	56.4	19.5	20.9	2.4
Lower-middle	1,001-2,000	21.7	35.5	50.0	13.0	0.8
Lower and slum	0-1,000	44.6	26.9	64.0	8.0	0.3
Total at 84 polls		100.0	40.8	44.6	12.6	1.2
Total Bogotá vote			39.9	45.0	13.0	1.2
II. Medellín: Voting in 24 Selected Polls (of 34 Total Polls)						
Upper		10.8	74.2	7.5	16.5	1.2
Middle		24.0	57.2	16.5	24.8	0.9
Lower		65.3	23.0	64.5	11.4	0.2
Total at 24 polls		100.0	36.7	46.9	15.2	0.4
Total Medellín vote			37.8	43.7	17.2	0.5

Source: Michael Brower, "Voting Patterns in Recent Colombian Elections," (Harvard University, Center for International Affairs, Unpublished paper, September 30, 1971).

depend, first, on the degree of urbanization (since even in 1970 class-based voting was significant only in the cities), and, secondly, on the extent to which the traditional parties offer alternatives to the voters. As has happened in other Latin American countries, when existing parties are confronted with the rise of the socio-economic base for class voting, they either have to realign themselves on a horizontal basis or must accept the probability that they will be displaced or supplemented on the political scene by parties that can establish class appeals. In the words of Robert Dix, commenting on the 1970 and 1974 elections, what is "most important for Colombia's developmental future has been the tilt in the axis of socio-political conflict from an essentially vertical one, between multi-class parties, *in the direction* of a horizontal, class-defined axis . . . . It seems unlikely that over the long term partisan competition in Colombia will wholly revert to its previous a-class nature."[28]

In Turkey, in the 1969 election, the more conservative Justice party lost votes in the more developed regions, but increased its vote in eight of the twenty least developed provinces. The Republican People's party, on the other hand, increased its vote in the more developed regions of the country and suffered significant losses in the more backward regions. This has been explained by the new "left-of-center" policy which the RPP inaugurated in the mid-1960s. This policy "represented a significant shift from the party's earlier elitist attitudes and its ambivalent positions on socio-economic issues to a more populist political style and a more coherent, reform-oriented, social democratic program with special emphasis on 'bread-and-butter' issues." The increase in the RPP vote in the more developed areas was explained by its increased support by the lower classes in those regions. The decline in the RPP vote in the more backward regions was due to the alienation from the party of the local elites in those regions and because "voting participation and party choices of the villagers are still largely guided and controlled by the traditional social elite." Paradoxically, the shift towards reform by RPP produced a decrease in its vote in those provinces where "the need for social reform remains most urgent."[29]

In the 1973 Turkish elections, the RPP increased its national vote substantially, but its gains were particularly marked in the urban *gecekondu* (shanty town) areas. It achieved this increase without any significant loss of votes in middle-class urban districts, and hence in 1973 it was able to show well-distributed multi-class support. It remains to be seen, however, how long it will be able to maintain the allegiance of the better-off elements in Turkish cities. For in the earlier elections the Justice party had been able to win support from the *gecekondu* residents through the appeals of patronage and concrete material benefits for individuals and neighborhoods. In 1973, however, the RPP appealed to the *gecekondu* neighborhoods on a class basis. The lesson of the 1973 elections, Özbuden argues, is that "with further socio-economic modernization and the increased political participation that goes with it, the bases of political participation shift from local community or urban neighborhood to social class, and individual-communal inducements tend to be replaced by sectoral (i.e., class) inducements."[30]

The spread of class-based voting does not necessarily mean that all classes automatically have their interests effectively articulated through class-based parties. In many countries, particularly in Latin America, parties have appealed to the economic interests of the upper, middle, and lower-middle classes, at the same time that no party has appealed to the lower classes other than in a desultory and pro forma way. In addition, the widespread prevalence of class-based voting in developed countries, and in the more developed regions of less developed countries, does not necessarily imply that socio-economic development leads to a predominance of class-based participation over other forms of participation. It is quite conceivable that lobbying, organizational activity, and some forms of contacting may continue to be pursued more on a neighborhood, communal group, or specialized economic group basis than on the basis of socio-economic class. The evidence available on this issue is simply too fragmentary for us to reach a judgment one way or another. Hence, all that can be done at this point is simply to emphasize that the spread of class-based voting participation as a result of socio-economic development does not in itself mean that all forms of political participation become class-based.

The Impact of Socio-Economic Equality on Political Participation

Socio-economic development thus does have the long-term effects of facilitating the expansion of political participation, diversifying the bases of participation, and substituting autonomous for mobilized participation. The validity of these relationships, which were assumed in the liberal model, is upheld, although the impact of development on participation is not necessarily immediate, direct, or entirely positive. The liberal model also assumed a positive causal relationship between socio-economic equality and political participation. That there is a relationship between equality and democracy is, of course, a familiar idea in the history of political thought, dating back to the Greeks. Great inequalities in wealth and status, it has been argued, are incompatible with a democratic system of government based on the concept of political equality. This idea was perhaps most explicitly formulated by de Tocqueville in his observations of how the "general equality of conditions" in America furnished the social basis for democracy in America. This proposition has the persuasiveness of an intuitive truth. It is, however, a proposition that presents some difficulties, so far as its systematic validation is concerned. First, the presumed dependent variable has generally been defined only as democratic political participation, not participation generally. This is appropriate if the object is to explain the presence or absence of democracy, but it is less useful if the object is to explain differences in overall levels, forms, and bases of participation. Second, the presumed independent variable is often left rather vaguely defined. Equality in what? Income? Wealth? Status? Equality of results or equality of opportunity? How can one measure equality and where can the data be found to construct indices of equality? Third, how can the presumed causal tie between the independent and dependent variables be demonstrated? How does one explain the relationship between these variables? Why should equality in one area of human life produce participation in another area? Is it not possible that the causal flow is from participation to equality rather than, as assumed, from equality to participation?

Perhaps because of these difficulties there has been relatively little systematic, empirical, comparative analysis relating equality to participation. There have, however, been efforts to test the Tocquevillian assumption of the relation between equality and democracy. Some studies suggest that there may be a significant relationship between the distribution of income and land ownership, on the one hand, and the presence or absence of democratic government, on the other. While a global association between economic equality and political democracy seems relatively clear, both of these variables also tend to correlate positively with levels of economic development. The question thus arises: To what extent is economic equality independently associated with political democracy? To determine this relationship, it is necessary to hold the level of economic development more or less constant. Two studies provide some data on this question.

(1) In 1964, Russett analyzed forty-seven countries during the 1950s in terms of their Gini index of inequality in land ownership and their classification in Lipset's categories of stable democracies, unstable democracies, and dictatorships. He found that: "Of the 23 states with the more equal pattern of land distribution, 13 are stable democracies, whereas only three of 24 more unequal countries can be classified as stable democracies." Hence, he concluded, de Tocqueville was right: "no state can long maintain a democratic form of government if the major

No Easy Choice

sources of economic gain are divided very unequally among its citizens. . . . A 'sturdy yeomanry' may be a virtual *sine qua non* for democratic government in an underdeveloped land."[31]

Russett points out that each of the three stable democracies (New Zealand, Uruguay, Australia) with greater than median inequality "is a fairly rich state where agriculture is no longer the principal source of wealth." The same, however, is even more true for the ten out of thirteen stable democracies with more than median equality. To some degree, in short, the results he presents could reflect a correlation between development and democracy rather than equality and democracy. To correct for this, it is desirable to limit the analysis to less developed countries, that is, for this purpose, those with forty percent or more of their labor force in agriculture. The results of this classification are presented in Table 3.2. All three stable democracies (India, the Philippines, Ireland) had greater than median equality; the unstable democracies were evenly divided; and the dictatorships (which comprise two-thirds of this sample) were tilted toward less equality. The overall relation between democracy and equality remained, although it was not nearly as dramatic and sharp as it was in the broader sample.

(2) In 1967, Cutright analyzed the relationships among intersectoral

Table 3.2. Inequality in Land Distribution

Gini index of inequality	Stable democracies		Unstable democracies		Dictatorships	
	Total	Less developed[a]	Total	Less developed	Total	Less developed
Greater than median equality	13	3	4	3	6	8
Median equality or less	3	0	8	3	13	11

SOURCE: Bruce M. Russett, "Inequality and Instability: The Relation of Land Tenure and Politics," *World Politics,* 16 (April 1964), pp. 442-54.

[a]Forty percent or more of labor force in agriculture.

income inequality, political representativeness, and economic development for forty-four noncommunist countries in the early 1950s. Twenty of the twenty-two countries with greater than median equality in income had democratic political systems; seventeen of the twenty-two with less than median equality had non-democratic systems. Cutright's political representation index had a zero order correlation of -0.63 with his index of income inequality.[32] Economic development was even more strongly related to democracy, but the tie between economic equality and democracy existed even when countries were divided according to levels of economic development. In the poorest category, three out of the four countries that had medium-high income-equality also had democratic systems of government, while all eight countries in the low income-equality group had nondemocratic systems.

The evidence presented so far shows that at the national level a broad correlation exists between economic equality and political democracy, a relation that generally holds up even when economic development is held constant. This does not prove that there is a relation between economic equality and political participation in general. Nor does it show the direction of the causal flow between equality and democracy. The first step in establishing the validity of the Tocquevillian hypothesis has been taken; we now turn to the second, or causal, proposition.

What grounds are there for thinking that economic equality furnishes

Table 3.3. Economic Development, Income Equality, and Democracy

Degree of income equality	Level of economic development							
	High (pcGNP > $800)		Medium (pcGNP-$300-799)		Low (pcGNP < $300)		Total	
	Dem.	Nondem.	Dem.	Nondem.	Dem.	Nondem.	Dem.	Nondem.
High	5	0	5	1	0	0	10	1
Medium High	5	0	2	0	3	1	10	1
Medium Low	2	0	0	2	2	5	4	7
Low	0	0	2	1	0	8	2	9
Total	12	0	9	4	5	14	26	18

SOURCE: Phillips Cutright, "Inequality: A Cross-National Analysis, *American Sociological Review,* 32 (August 1967), pp. 562ff.

an impetus to political democracy? One approach clearly is to look at historical sequences in the evolution of societies. Which came first: economic equality or political democracy? Little comparative work has been done on this issue, with the major exception of Sunshine's study of the relation between economic equality and the development of political democracy in nineteenth and early twentieth century Europe. His data suggest that the critical breakthrough in the introduction of democratic institutions took place after a society had evolved in the direction of greater income equality, and that this breakthrough was then followed by an acceleration of the tendency toward income equality.[33] In short, the assumptions of both the liberal and the populist models about the causal flows between these variables are correct at different phases in the evolution of societies.

An alternative way of establishing causal links between economic equality and political participation (in a democratic or undemocratic society) is by linking "objective" economic conditions to "subjective" attitudes, which in turn affect "objective" political behavior. Economic development, for instance, has been shown to increase the diversity of socio-economic statuses in society and to increase the proportion of higher status positions. At the individual level, higher status is associated with feelings of greater political efficacy, and efficacy, in turn, leads to higher levels of political participation. Conceivably, greater equality in status may also have a marked impact on the sense of political efficacy that the average citizen has in a society and hence on participation. The literature analyzing the relation of the sense of efficacy to participation has generally left unresolved, however, the question of the relative importance of *absolute* political efficacy vis-à-vis the political system (that is, knowledge about politics, perceptions of the relevance of politics to one's needs, and the like) and *relative* political efficacy vis-à-vis other participants in the system (that is, feelings of superior or inferior interpersonal competence).[34] Is it primarily the *level* of status or the *equality* of status that produces the feelings of efficacy that lead, in turn, to political participation?

Education, for instance, promotes a sense of political efficacy and higher levels of political participation. But at what educational level would a society have the highest levels of political participation?

Level of education	Percent of total population	
	Society A	Society B
None	0%	0%
Elementary	50	100
Secondary	25	0
College	25	0

Society A clearly has a higher average educational level than Society B. If one assumes that elementary education produces a certain general level of political participation, and that secondary and higher education produce higher levels of participation, then Society A obviously will have more participation than Society B. However, the feelings of political efficacy (and the participation level) of the fifty percent of the population with an elementary education in Society A could be significantly less than the felt efficacy (and participation level) of the overall population in Society B. The elementary school educated of Society A might in fact be equally sophisticated concerning knowledge of the political system and its perceived relevance, but they might well feel less efficacious than their B counterparts because of the superior education of the other fifty percent of the population in Society A. Correspondingly, the twenty-five percent with higher education in Society A might feel considerably more competent than, say, the total population of a Society C, all of whom were college educated, simply because of their superiority in education to the other three quarters of Society A.

If the logic of this analysis holds up, a society with more equal, but lower average, levels of status might have higher levels of political participation than a society with less equal, but higher average, levels of status. This could be one explanation of why American cities with more highly educated populations have lower voting turnouts than those with less well educated citizens.[35] It also ties in with Powell's interesting finding that high levels of voting turnout, as well as of solidarity in voting preferences, were prevalent in two types of peasant villages: "when there is a high degree of inequality in landholding patterns and dominance by one or very few large landlords, and at the other extreme when there is a very low degree of landholding inequality, and the corporate village pattern is approximated."[36] In the villages with great economic inequality, the high turnouts are clearly the product of mobilized participation, which "is an integral part of the patron-client exchange process." In the corporate village pattern, coercion may, as Powell stresses, play a significant role; but the high levels of participation also undoubtedly express an autonomous recognition of similar opportunities and interests flowing from equality of circumstances.

Status equality is most likely to lead to high levels of political participation when the perception of that equality is widespread, and when there is a perceived threat to people in one status from people in another status, that is, in Marxist terms, under conditions of class consciousness and class conflict. Under these conditions, participation is the product of feelings of equal political efficacy among the members of the status group and of the group's feeling of collective efficacy vis-a-vis other status groups. These conditions, for instance, are likely to be present in an urban squatter settlement shortly before and after a successful land invasion: objective equality of condition would be supplemented by subjective perception of that equality, by the perception of a probable threat to their status, and by awareness of the possibilities of political action to secure that status.

The liberal model of development assumes that economic development has a positive effect on both economic equality and political participation, and that economic equality has an additional independent positive effect on participation. But it has now been established that high rates of economic development often have a negative effect on economic equality. However, the evidence presented in this and the previous section suggests that, in some measure, the positive relationships may still hold between development and equality, on the one hand, and between both these variables and participation, on the other. To the extent that this is the case, the question we posed at the beginning of this chapter arises again: What is the overall impact of economic development on political participation? Does the long-term positive result of development, in terms of the broadening of political participation, counterbalance in scope, or supplant in time, the perhaps shorter-term negative impact that it may have by reducing economic equality and thus reducing participation? What are the consequences for participation of a pattern of development that promotes more rapid economic development at the expense of increasing economic inequality, as compared to a policy that gives first priority to insuring a more equitable distribution of

Table 3.4. Distribution of Income

	Chad	Colombia	USA	44 LDCs
Poorest fifth	12%	3%	5%	6%
Next fifth	11	6	11	8
Next fifth	12	10	16	12
Next fifth	22	18	23	19
Richest fifth	43	63	46	56
Richest 5%	23	34	20	30

SOURCE: Irma Adelman and Cynthia Taft Morris, "An Anatomy of Patterns of Income Distribution in Developing Nations," Part III, Final Report, Grant AID/csd-2236, February 12, 1971; Michael Brower, "Income Distribution in Colombia and Other Selected Countries" (Harvard University, Center for International Affairs, March 1971).

the fruits of development, at the price of a slower overall rate of economic growth? In terms of the distribution of statuses in society, will political participation best be promoted by status elevation or status equalization?

As the evidence presented above suggests, both variables have some positive effect on participation, although little if any work has been done on their relative impact. Political democracy, however, appears to be more strongly related to economic development than to economic equality, and somewhat the same relation may prevail between these economic variables and political participation more generally. It is, for instance, recognized that economic equality, and presumably equality in other status variables, is higher in societies at the lowest and highest levels of economic development than it is in societies at middle levels of development. Although there may be exceptions, overall levels of participation tend to reflect levels of socio-economic development, largely as a result of the changes that development produces in the distribution of socio-economic statuses. The distribution of income in Chad, for instance, resembles to a striking degree the distribution of income in the United States (except that the poorest fifth of the population is relatively better off in Chad). Income distribution in both countries contrasts with the much more unequal pattern in Colombia. Yet it would seem likely that there are higher levels of political participation in Colombia than in Chad, and higher levels in the United States than in Colombia. The U-shaped relationship between economic equality and socio-economic development contrasts with the relatively linear relationship between political participation and socio-economic development. To the extent that the causal flow is from the economic to the political variables, status level would appear to be more decisive than status equality in influencing political participation.

The Impact of Participation on Development and Equality

So far we have discussed the strength of the relation between the economic variables—development and equality—on the one hand, and participation, on the other, and how the causal flow might run from the former to the latter. This is in keeping, of course, with our concern throughout this study with political participation as a dependent variable. The evidence for an *association* between political participation and the economic variables is, however, considerably stronger than the evidence for the presumed *causal* relationship between the two. It might, consequently, be instructive to reverse the causal assumption and to consider at this point the influence that the expansion of political participation may have on socio-economic development and socio-economic equality. As we have suggested, there is reason to believe that this relationship may change according to the level of overall modernization or development of the society. At higher levels of development, the expansion of political participation along the lines of the populist model is associated with greater socio-economic equality and less attention to economic growth. Conversely, in the technocratic model, high rates of economic growth and less attention to questions of equity are associated with the suppression of political participation. In the earlier phases of development, on the other hand, the expansion of political participation is associated with less socio-economic equality. In these early phases, however, both the low levels of political participation characteristic of the autocratic model and the higher levels of middle-class participation found in the bourgeois model may be compatible with high rates of economic growth.

That higher levels of political participation should have positive effects on socio-economic equality seems a plausible assumption. If economic development has a "natural" tendency to enhance economic inequality, strong governmental action will be necessary to counteract this trend. Such governmental action is likely to be the product of the expansion of political participation, or at least to require the simultaneous expansion of participation if it is to be successfully implemented. More generally, widespread political participation generally means more widespread access to political power, and those who gain access to power will insist that the government act to broaden their share in the economic benefits of society.

The political history of Western societies in the late nineteenth and early twentieth centuries can be written largely in terms of, first, the growth of democracy and the expansion of political participation to the lower classes, and, later, the increasing role of the state as the promoter of economic and social welfare. As has been pointed out, Sunshine found that the broadening of the suffrage in western European societies was preceded by a trend toward greater income equality and was followed by the acceleration of that trend. In his analysis of income distribution, Cutright found that political representativeness was second only to the level of economic development in explaining the variance among countries.[37] More directly to the point, he also found the extent of a country's social security programs to be most powerfully related to its level of economic development. When the latter was controlled for, however, the evidence showed that more representative governments provided earlier and greater social security coverage to their populations than less representative governments. In addition, in economically more developed countries, the innovation of new social security programs tended to follow positive changes in political representativeness. Consequently, when the effects of economic development were held constant, the analysis generally supported the hypothesis that "governments in nations whose political structures tend to allow for greater accessibility to the people of the governing elite will act to provide greater social security for their populations than that provided by governments whose rulers are less accessible to the demands of the population."[38] In a similar vein, Adelman and Morris conclude that while "greater economic participation does not lead to greater political participation," there is "some evidence that greater political participation tends to lead to a more egalitarian distribution of the national product."[39]

Where competitive elections are one of the channels of political participation, they also tend to produce a broader distribution of material benefits by the government. In Kenya, for instance, despite the government's use of both the carrot and the stick to limit participation, the fact that national leaders "had to fight elections meant that they had to go to their constituents to renew support." Kenya's system of factional politics is "responsive to popular pressure" because it "can deliver goods and services which are highly valued and it can provide for turnover in the individuals who represent without actually altering the relationship between elites and non-elites."[40] Electoral competition may also enable squatters and others among the urban poor to induce governmental elites and ruling parties to respond to their material needs. In Turkey, legislation designed to cut back or to prohibit squatter settlements or *gecekondus* generally has little effect

> since the ways in which the *gecekondu* laws are locally implemented are often determined by political considerations. Neither the national government nor the municipal authorities have shown much courage or inclination to enforce such laws strictly. It has often been observed that in the weeks preceding national or local elections, *gecekondu*-dwellers were given at least verbal assurances of legalization, and that such times were the most intense periods of construction. Political considerations also play an important part in the installation and funding of municipal services in the *gecekondu* areas. The mayor of one of the largest cities reportedly keeps a record of the votes for his party in each precinct and allocates the funds on the basis of their party loyalties.[41]

In addition to the collective benefits that voting can bring to particular neighborhoods, the vote can also be used to produce a broader distribution of economic rewards among individuals. In Izmir in Turkey, for instance, party leaders "more or less frequently performed for their supporters such services as obtaining credits, finding employment, and aiding in their dealings with governmental authorities." Fifty-three percent of the local leaders of the Justice party said they often helped their constituents find jobs, while an additional thirty-one percent did so from time to time.[42] In Latin American cities where competitive party politics prevails, urban squatters employ similar vote-trading tactics, although community leaders may eventually shift to direct lobbying with governmental officials.[43] By and large, the evidence from recent studies reinforces that from earlier ones: political participation via the ballot is a potent weapon of the urban poor in achieving higher levels of certain material benefits and thus in helping to reduce economic inequality.

All this suggests a high degree of validity for the populist model's assumption that the degree of economic equality in a society is largely a direct function of the scope of the political participation in that society. The extent to which this proposition is true, however, varies with the overall level of development, economic and political, of the society. In fact, in the early stages of development, the expansion of political participation tends to have a negative impact on economic equality; this effect is contrary to the assumptions of the liberal, technocratic, and populist models. The inauguration of the process of economic development increases economic inequality, particularly in the countryside, as population densities increase and more peasants are displaced from the land. The growth of cities gives rise to a small but active urban middle class. In the absence of strong, centralized, autocratic power, the society is then likely to develop along the lines of the bourgeois model. The urban middle class asserts itself politically and joins the traditional (usually rural-based) elite as a participant in the political process. The urban middle class then employs its new weight in politics to improve its own economic position, and this gives rise to a widening gap between urban and rural standards of living. *In effect, during this period, both the process of economic development and the expansion of political participation combine to increase economic inequality.* Only subsequently, when the expansion of political participation reaches the peasantry and the urban working class, does that expansion begin to have a more positive effect on economic equality. Thus, the assumption of the populist (and implicitly of the technocratic) model that participation and equality are positively related is true only at certain stages in the developmental process.

The inverse relation between participation and equality in the earlier stages of development is clearly revealed in the conditions under which meaningful land reform is most likely to take place. While more competitive and participatory political systems are generally more likely to promote economic equality in later phases of development, the evidence is overwhelming that land reform—one of the most dramatic ways of enhancing both status equality and status level in rural society—is more likely to be introduced effectively by noncompetitive and nondemocratic governments.[44] Land reform, if it is to have a meaningful impact on development, must occur in the earlier phases of the developmental process. If it is to occur at that point, however, political participation must be limited. If participation has expanded to the point where medium sized landowners play an active role in politics, land reform becomes difficult or impossible. Parliaments are the enemy of land reform, and a modest body of political participants is likely to have the interest and the means to obstruct the approval and implementation of such reforms. What is needed for reform in these circumstances is the limitation of participation and the centralization of power in an autocratic ruler.

Some further evidence of the impact that a modest expansion of political participation has on economic inequality can be seen in the Adelman and Morris data on income distribution in forty-four less developed countries. These countries can be roughly classified as pro-rich or anti-rich, according to whether the richest five percent of their population gets more or less than thirty percent of the total income. They can also be classified as pro-poor or anti-poor, according to whether the poorest twenty percent of the population gets more or less than five percent of the total income. If this breakdown of countries is analyzed according to the nature of their political systems, it becomes clear that the nondemocratic countries are more likely to be pro-rich and pro-poor while the democratic societies tend to be anti-rich and anti-poor. Sixty-nine percent of the democratic countries and forty-five percent of the nondemocratic ones have anti-rich income distributions; sixty-one percent of the democratic countries also have an anti-poor income distribution, compared to forty-five percent of the nondemocratic countries. Thirty-eight percent of the democratic countries, but only ten percent of the nondemocratic ones, have income distributions that are both anti-poor and anti-rich. In less developed countries, in short, democratic institutions enhance the power of the middle class and make the poor as well as the rich worse off than they are likely to be in nondemocratic societies.

The positive relation that we have postulated between expansion of political participation to middle-class groups and increasing income inequality is also supported by Verba and Nie's analysis of the relationship between participation and responsiveness of political leaders in sixty-four American communities. They measured responsiveness in terms of the degree of concurrence between leaders and citizens on the major problems confronting the community. They also had a composite index of the level of political participation in the communities. One might expect that there would be a straight linear relationship between participation and responsiveness (or concurrence), but in fact this turns out not to be the case. The highest levels of responsiveness do indeed coincide with the highest levels of participation; but the overall relation is a curvilinear one, with political leaders in communities with the lowest levels of participation being more responsive than the leaders in communities with slightly higher levels of participation. Communities in the next to the lowest quartile of participation have the political leaders least responsive to the overall views of the citizens. The reason for this is that political leaders are primarily responsive to political participants. If a relatively small and unrepresentative portion of the community is politically active, the views, and presumably the actions, of the political

Table 3.5.   Income Distribution and Type of Political System

| Poorest 20% share of income | Richest 5% share of income | | | | | |
| | Less than 30% | | More than 30% | | Total | |
	Dem.	Nondem.	Dem.	Nondem.	Dem.	Nondem.
Less than 5%	5	3	3	11	8	14
More than 5%	4	11	1	6	5	17
Total	9	14	4	17	13	31

SOURCE: Adelman and Morris, "An Anatomy of Patterns of Income Distribution in Developing Nations," Part III, Final Report, Grant AID/csd-2236, February 12, 1971.

leaders will reflect the interests of that constituency. If, on the other hand, virtually no one is politically participant, political leaders are freer to maintain their own views on community problems, which are more likely to correspond more closely with those of the citizens at large.[45] They are able to think in terms of the whole community rather than simply a small part of it. A little participation, in short, is an unrepresentative thing.

To summarize: political participation and socio-economic equality interact. But, contrary to assumptions of the liberal model, the flow of causal influence is stronger from political participation to socio-economic equality than in the reverse direction. In its early phases, the expansion of political participation along the lines of the bourgeois model tends to promote greater socio-economic inequality, thus reinforcing the effect of economic development. In its later phases, the expansion of political participation tends, in accordance with the operations of the populist model, to promote greater socio-economic equality through governmental action to redistribute income and wealth.

Mobility, Organization, and Participation

Participation at the Micro Level

The preceding chapter considered the relation between development, equality, and participation at the macro or societal level. In this chapter, attention is shifted from the overall characteristics of a society, and the choices which it confronts as a society, to the "micro" level of the individual and the group context in which he operates. The focus is on the choices that may or may not be open to individuals, singly and in groups, to choose political participation or some other means of achieving their objectives. In some measure, the analysis in this chapter parallels on the individual level the analysis made in Chapter Three on the societal level.

In Chapter Three it was argued that one assumption of the liberal model of development does remain generally valid: Increasing levels of socio-economic development are associated with broader, more diverse, and more autonomous patterns of political participation. In this chapter, we will explore the operation of this interrelationship, and its presumed causal connection, at the individual level. How does a higher level of socio-economic development within a society give rise to higher levels of political participation by specific individuals and groups in that society? Development increases overall status levels and organizational complexity in a society. Higher socio-economic status and more organizational involvement lead to more political participation. Indeed, in a reanalysis of the Almond and Verba data, Nie and his associates show that the effects of economic development on political participation are entirely mediated through socio-economic status and organizational involvement.[1] Improvements in socio-economic status are often the product of individual mobility; organizational involvement is the product of group consciousness and identification.

The socio-economic development of a society thus creates two channels that can eventually lead to increased political participation—the mobility channel and the organizational channel. Our concern in this chapter is how each channel operates to increase participation, how it affects the nature of the resulting participation, and how movement through one channel preempts, encourages, or leads to movement through the other. We will consider first the mobility channel to higher socio-economic status, then the organizational channel, and finally the relations between the two as alternative and sequential routes to participation.

Socio-Economic Status and Political Participation

Modern societies have higher levels of political participation than traditional societies, in part because of differences in status structure. The socio-economic development of a society leads to a fairly linear increase in the status level of the society and to a curvilinear change in status equality in the society. (See Chapter Three.) In more economically developed societies, more people have higher incomes, more wealth, better education, and more highly skilled occupations. These factors obviously correlate very strongly with each other. But studies indicate that each factor also tends to have an independent effect of varying strength on political participation. In general, income appears to be very strongly related to political participation, and education even more strongly. The turnout figures (Table 4.1) for the 1970 presidential election in Colombia are typical of the effects of income differences. In his study of working-class men in six nations, Inkeles found education to have a consistently high relation to active citizenship when other variables, such as factory experience, rural or urban origin, media consumption, and length of urban residence, were held constant. Length of factory experience also had a consistent, if less strong, relationship to active citizenship in all six countries. On the average, each additional year of education added about 2.5 points to an individual's active participation score (rated from 0 to 100), while each additional year of factory work added about 1.25 points. Similarly, Almond and Verba concluded that: "Among the demographic variables usually investigated—sex, place of residence, occupation, income, age, and so on—none compares with the educational variable in the extent to which

Table 4.1. Voting Turnout and Income Level: 1970 Presidential Election in Bogotá, Colombia

Socio-economic level of barrio	Approximate income level (pesos/mo.)	% Adult population voting (post-election survey)
Upper	Over 10,000	85%
Upper-middle	5,001 - 10,000	94
Middle	2,001 - 5,000	76
Lower-middle	1,001 - 2,000	67
Lower & slum	0 - 1,000	59

Source: Michael Brower, "Voting Patterns in Recent Colombian Elections" (Unpublished paper, Harvard University, Center for International Affairs, September 30, 1971).

it seems to determine political attitudes." Education and other status variables are, however, more clearly related to some forms of political participation than to others. In the Verba-Nie five-nation study, for instance, education showed a strong relationship with both campaign activity and communal activity, a weak relationship with voting, and virtually no relationship with particularized contacting.[2]

Why do status variables tend to produce greater political participation? The overwhelming evidence from a variety of studies indicates that high status is associated with feelings of political efficacy and competence, and that those who feel politically efficacious are much more likely to participate in politics than those who do not. The status variables, in short, are related to participation through attitudinal variables. Indeed, high-status individuals who do not feel politically efficacious do not participate in politics significantly more than similarly inefficacious low-status individuals.[3] In addition, higher-status people, particularly highly educated people, are more likely to feel that it is the duty of a citizen to participate in politics, and people who have this sense of duty do, in fact, participate more.[4]

The extent to which the status model functions through subjective feelings of competence and efficacy is underlined by the apparent deviations from the model, where high-status people do not participate as fully as they should. On the basis of ecological analysis, for instance, a high correlation was found between education (measured by percent literate) and voting turnout in Philippine presidential elections from 1953 to 1965. In 1953, for instance, the correlation was .707. In the 1949 presidential election, however, there was a negative relationship of -.268 between literacy and turnout. What accounts for this deviation from the norm? The explanation, it has been suggested, may be that in 1949 the more highly educated citizen believed that he could *not* be efficacious. The 1949 election was conducted in an atmosphere of seemingly massive fraud and corruption, which would lead the better educated citizen to believe that his vote would not be worth anything. "For any system of choice, the decision maker must perceive some purpose for his choice behavior. If the decision maker (in this case the citizen as voter) does not perceive any purpose to his activity he will cease to manifest that activity; only the obstinate or the ignorant repeat an activity which does not reward them."[5]

A somewhat similar inverse relationship between level of education and voting turnout occurred among urban Chinese in the 1964 Malayan elections. This happened, it has been explained, because the "Malayan Chinese have been systematically discriminated against, disfranchised or otherwise reduced to a low level of political efficacy." As a result, "increased levels of education among Chinese in urban Malaya lead to an awareness that one's vote is meaningless."[6] Less well-educated Chinese, like the less well-educated Filipinos in 1949, were less aware of the decreased efficacy of their vote and consequently maintained higher levels of voting.

In India, polling data from 1961, 1964, and 1967 indicate that more highly educated people were more interested in politics, discussed politics more frequently, and made more efforts to influence decisions by local or national governmental authorities, that is, they more often engaged in contacting or lobbying activity. The same polls, however, show that the more highly educated were less likely to engage in electoral activity, including voting, attending political meetings, and contributing money to political campaigns. The highest levels of electoral participation were reached by those with some elementary education, followed closely by illiterates, and then by the high-school educated, with the college-educated having the lowest rates of participation. In all three forms of electoral activity the college-educated participated less than the illiterates.

Three explanations have been suggested.[7] First, voting requires time and effort, which the more educated were less willing to spend than the poorly educated, for whom voting may be a festive occasion. Second, group pressures, group appeals to caste loyalties, and bribes may produce substantial mobilized participation in electoral activities by the less educated, while not having the same effect on the more educated. Finally, other survey data suggest that the more highly educated may be more alienated from the political system and from governmental policies (at least in the early 1960s). In India, the more highly educated were more clearly in favor of communism, authoritarian government, and army rule than the less educated, who were more favorably disposed towards the existing democratic system dominated by the Congress party. This alienation of the educated may have been the result of the "provincialization" of Indian politics in the two decades after independence, the emergence of a mass political culture, and the extent to which politicians found that "appeals to caste, communal, and provincial factors pay off at the polls."[8]

The democratization of politics thus may lead to a withdrawal of higher-status groups from politics, because their participation is a function of their feelings of efficacy and they feel inefficacious in attempting to influence politics dominated by low-status actors and low-status styles of behavior. One wonders, for instance, whether this relative failure of highly educated Indians to vote, attend political meetings, and contribute money to campaigns may not have had its parallel in the United States in the 1830s and 1840s, when electoral participation expanded, populist appeals multiplied, and political leaders of lower-status backgrounds began to play more prominent roles. In many developing countries, the prospect of mass participation by the lower classes has led to military coups designed to veto that development.[9] In India, and in the United States, this result was avoided, but a price may still have been paid in the alienation and withdrawal, at least partial and possibly temporary, of higher-status groups from their normal participation in, and support for, the political system.

Most studies relating status to participation have focused on the role of income, education, and occupation. There are, however, scattered indications of the importance of another set of factors involving economic independence and dependence. Among the important variables here are home ownership vs. rental residence, land ownership vs. tenancy for farmers, and whether the source of income is from within or without the relevant political constituency. In their study of four Wisconsin cities, Alford and Scoble found home ownership to be a major determinant of local political participation, along with socio-economic status and organizational involvement.[10] In rural Colombia, the political efficacy of peasants is not related to the traditional forms of political participation as client in a patron-client relationship, that is, to what we would describe as mobilized participation. Nor is it related to exposure to the mass media. Instead, it is associated with land tenure. The "efficacious peasants are the small-holders," who own their own land, and who are "relatively more independent of the landlord and the agricultural resources he controls." Thus "the small-holder is somehow insulated from the sense of powerlessness and resignation which infects other strata of the peasantry."[11] In rural areas land ownership is generally a prerequisite to autonomous political participation. Thus, in central Brazil, nonowners are virtually excluded "from social and political participation" and hence are dependent on the "more privileged community members to serve as brokers in their relations with the rest of the system."[12]

The relatively high levels of orthodox political participation found in many urban migrant communities may have developed because the migrants are squatters who, through one means or another, become at least *de facto* land and home owners. The need to legitimize this situation provides a major incentive for political action, and the achievement of such legitimacy may provide the basis for a sense of political efficacy and community involvement. In Lima, for instance, voting and party participation were higher in the squatter settlements than in the largely rental slum areas, a relationship that held when variables such as age and sex were controlled. Similarly, in Turkish cities, the voting turnout rates in the *gecekondu* or squatter settlements did not differ significantly from those for better-off areas of the city. One reason may be that low levels of income were compensated for by high levels of home ownership. In Ankara, seventy-two percent of the residents of traditional central portions of the city ("old Ankara") were tenants as against only thirty-one percent of those in the *gecekondu* neighborhoods.[13] For major Turkish cities generally, a majority of *gecekondu* residents are homeowners.

Along similar lines, Lester Salamon has shown that black voting in Mississippi counties in the 1960s was related not to levels of economic development or to levels of black income, but rather to the extent to which Negroes had sources of income relatively independent of control by the local whites. Black voting participation was highest in those counties where there were substantial numbers of self-employed blacks and in those counties along the state border where substantial numbers of blacks worked in factories and other places of employment in Louisiana.[14] More generally, the early expansion of political participation in the United States in the 1820s and 1830s may have come about because the widespread ownership of land not only enabled many to meet the property requirements for voting but also created the social-economic-psychological bases for voting. A population that was composed substantially (as it was) of "free farmers," in Dahl's sense of the word, should have been characterized by widespread feelings of political efficacy and should have had widespread political participation (as it did).[15]

Group Consciousness and Political Participation

People who are members of organizations and participate actively in them are also much more likely to participate in politics. In Mexico City, for instance, urban migrants "who had participated in community improvement organizations were *five times* more likely to have engaged in [political] demandmaking than the nonparticipants." Similar results have been reported for low-income communities in Santiago, Chile, and Lima, Peru.[16] Indeed, an increasing amount of evidence suggests that organizational involvement may be more important than socio-economic status in explaining differences in political participation. A careful reanalysis of the Almond-Verba data for the United States, Great Britain, Germany, Italy, and Mexico shows that while socio-economic status explains roughly ten percent of the variance in participation, organizational involvement explains roughly twenty-five percent of that variance. Other studies have suggested similar conclusions.[17]

If organizational involvement tends to increase political participation, the next question is: what produces organizational involvement? As suggested above, the increased participation of individuals in organized groups is, by and large, a function of economic development. How, then, does economic development increase organizational involvement? There would appear to be two distinct routes: one via socio-economic status and another, more direct, via group consciousness.

In most countries there is a tendency for people with higher education, income, and occupational status to be more involved in organizations than people with less of these attributes. This relationship is much more striking in some countries than in others, and it is particularly striking in the United States. In 1955, eighty-two percent of Americans in the highest of five socio-economic classes belonged to organizations, as compared with only eight percent of those in the lowest class. Erbe's study of three Iowa communities found social status and organizational involvement to be more closely related to each other than either factor was to political participation.[18] Organizational activity varies directly with education in the United States but not in Norway.[19] More generally, Nie and his associates found the following product-moment correlation coefficients between social status and organizational involvement in five countries:[20]

United States	.435
United Kingdom	.313
Italy	.304
Mexico	.227
Germany	.213

These results suggest that there may be substantial differences between societies in the degree of association between social status and organizational involvement. A close relationship between organizational involvement and social status tends to reinforce class distinctions in political participation. In societies where other factors, such as class or group consciousness, may be responsible for organizational involvement, such involvement may counterbalance the dampening effect of social status on political participation by low-status people. Thus, the less rigid the class structure of a society, the more important are class and status differences in explaining differences in participation. The more rigid the class structure of a society, and the greater the class or group consciousness of the lower status population, the less political participation tends to be related to socio-economic status, provided that low-status group participation is not held down by either political repression or a "negative" self-image by the group that it "should not" participate in politics. Class rigidity thus leads to group consciousness and political participation only in societies where other conditions permit political activity by low-status groups.

The differences between the United States and Sweden in voting participation by occupational class are, perhaps, indicative of these relationships. In the United States there is a very strong correlation between occupational status and voting. In Sweden there is virtually no relationship: the group consciousness and organizational involvement of the lower classes counteracts the effects of socio-economic status on political participation (See Figure 4.1.)

Organizational involvement as a result of group consciousness appears to affect political participation in rather different ways than socio-economic status does. Status, as we have indicated, promotes participation primarily through changes in attitudes about politics. Organizational involvement, on the other hand, tends to produce increased participation without any significant change in attitudes. In the re-analysis of the Almond-Verba data, sixty percent of the political participation attributable to social status was found to have come about through changes in attitudes: an increased sense of the duty to participate, more political information, greater perceived impact of government on individual interests, greater political efficacy, more political attentiveness. Sixty percent of the political participation resulting from organizational involvement, by contrast, was the product of a direct relationship, without intervention of the attitude variables.[21] In somewhat the same fashion, the mobilization of Venezuelan peasants into unions and political parties occurred before the peasants had developed feelings of political efficacy. This mobilization produced high rates of political participation, which, in turn, led the peasants to develop feelings of political efficacy.[22] Similarly, migrants to Mexico City were found to be much more involved in "community-based political activity" and to have voted more often than native-born residents, although the latter scored much higher on cognitive involvement in the political process. The behavioral participation of the migrants in politics was largely independent of high levels of political information, supportive psychological orientations or other kinds of traits or resources com-

No Easy Choice

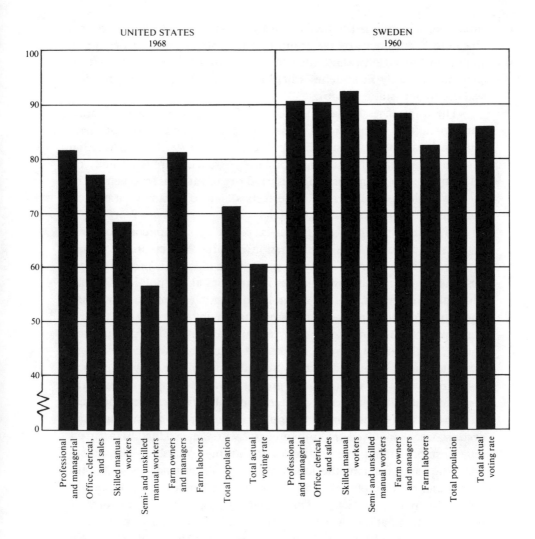

Figure 4.1 Voting Participation Rates by Occupation

Source: Based on survey data reported in Walter Dean Burnham, "A Political Scientist and Voting-Rights Litigation: The Case of the 1966 Texas Registration Statute," *Washington University Law Quarterly* (Spring 1971), pp. 356-57. As Professor Burnham notes, the gap of 10.5% between those who said they voted and the actual voting rate in the United States in 1968 means that the difference in voting rates between high status and low status occupations was undoubtedly even greater than these survey figures show.

monly assumed to be requisites for sustained political participation.[23] This is consistent with the findings of a variety of other studies, which "have also shown that organizational involvement may lead to increased political participation *in the absence* of other personal attributes or attitudes such as high socio-economic status, a sense of political efficacy, or a high level of political information."[24]

The involvement of low-status people in organizations is likely to result from the development of a distinct sense of group consciousness. The group may be a class, a communal group, or a neighborhood. The more intensely the individual identifies with the group, the more likely he is to be organizationally involved and politically participant. In the United States, for instance, "blacks who identify as members of an ethnic community tend to participate more actively in most areas than do nonidentifiers . . . . " and hence "membership in a cohesive ethnic community does propel many individuals toward participation in a variety of social and political arenas."[25] Group consciousness among blacks, indeed, produced rates of political participation equal to those among whites, despite differences in average socio-economic status.[26] Similarly, one would expect the empirical evidence to support Pizzorno's proposition that "political participation increases with the increase in class consciousness."[27] On the neighborhood level, Cornelius found that the "single most important determinant of frequency of political participation among migrants is a general disposition to work collectively, i.e., a generalized preference for collectively rather than individually pursued solutions to salient personal and community-related problems." Such a disposition, in turn, "enhances the level and quality of participation in community-based voluntary organizations, participation which, in turn, strengthens individual predispositions toward involvement in other forms of political activity."[28] Thus, class, communal, and neighborhood consciousness all seem to have positive consequences for organizational involvement and political participation.

It is, consequently, less the characteristics of individuals than the group context in which they find themselves that shapes the participation patterns of low-status persons in both rural and urban areas. The residential environment in particular, whether a village or an urban barrio, constitutes an "important arena for political learning." As a result, "persons with the same set of individual attributes may participate politically in significantly varying degree, depending on the proportion of those within their immediate social environment who are politically active or who share some perception or attitudinal trait relevant to political activity."[29] In a similar vein, Powell has argued that the political implications of peasant organizational involvement must be found in the "concrete *context* of union participation. . . ."[30] The individual, in short, will tend to conform to the political norms of his community. Whatever his socio-economic characteristics, he will be participant if the community generally is participant. Hence, "given sufficient opportunity for political learning, together with strong community leadership and organizational support, the urban poor may participate more frequently than those at considerably higher levels of the social hierarchy."[31]

The question then becomes: What generates the group consciousness that makes a community a participant community? Two factors seem to be most relevant: First, experiences involving intense or sustained conflict or challenges to the group's existence may intensify group identification and give rise to sustained patterns of political participation. High voting rates in West Virginia in the 1960s, for instance, have been explained by the history of conflict from the 1890s through the 1920s, when "the state was an open battleground in the effort to unionize its miners. Contrary to what was taking place in other border and southern states, in West Virginia that group which was least likely to participate in politics—the lower socio-economic status group, the 'working man'—was being motivated and 'organized' to participate." This participation, and the motivation behind it, were given organizational embodiment in the coalition between the miners' unions and the Democratic party; over the years this coalition "contrived to foster the active political participation of the lower socio-economic status group."[32] Similarly, the disposition of urban migrants in Mexico City to work collectively is largely a product of urban socialization experiences, particularly collective politicizing experiences such as land invasions, confrontation with the police, government agencies, landowners, or other authority figures, and other types of experiences culminating in "negative sanctions."[33] Such collective experiences, generating group consciousness, may stimulate a political culture or style favorable to participation, which may continue for years after the initial formative experience. In other circumstances, however, sustained high-level group identification and political participation may require sustained external conflict. The political participation of squatters in new urban settlements, for instance, often declines after the community has become securely established and external conflicts have lessened. Similarly, in American cities conflict among ethnic groups produces higher rates of political participation by the members of those groups.[34]

A second critical factor enhancing group consciousness and participation is the insulation of the members of the group from outside influences and contacts that might create competing affiliations and loyalties. It has been demonstrated in a variety of contexts that individuals subject to cross-pressures are less likely to vote, or otherwise to participate politically, than those free of such cross-pressures. Hence, when a community is more homogeneous and members of a group have contact only with each other, the rates of political participation are higher. Manual workers participate much more extensively in community affairs in communities that lack middle-class residents than they do in more heterogeneous communities with significant middle-class populations.[35] Many years ago, Tingsten generalized this tendency into what he labeled the "law of the social centre of gravity" to the effect that "electoral participation within a group rises with the relative strength of the group in the electoral district." A variety of evidence from several countries supports this proposition.[36] Other things being equal, the more segregated a group is, the more politically participant are its members. In Lane's formulation, the tendency of members of a group to participate in politics depends on: the proportion of the group to the total population of the voting district (the proportion effect); the degree of concentration of the members of the group in a voting district (the concentration effect); and the extent to which group members in a voting district feel they are different from the surrounding population (the enclave effect).[37]

In his analysis of village voting patterns Powell found a somewhat similar effect. Evidence from a variety of studies shows "two contrasting patterns of voting behavior" in villages. In one pattern, there is very high turnout plus "village-wide solidarity and homogeneity in turnout and voting preferences." In the other, there is lower turnout plus "great variation and factionalism in terms of participation and voting preferences."

The high solidarity-high turnout syndrome could be found where there was great inequality in landowning, with a single patron mobilizing his supporters to the polls, or in the corporate village pattern, with high equality in land ownership and a mixture of coercion and social pressure insuring compliance with group norms.[38]

Participation in urban communities is shaped by similar variables. Greater socio-economic homogeneity in a community facilitates the recognition of mutual interests and the development of cooperative political behavior. The isolation of the community from external political influences also encourages higher levels of participation. On the other hand, when "supra local interests and concerns become the dominant influence in 'community' activities, resident participation usually declines. . . ."[39]

In line with the effects of insulation and an absence of cross-pressures, participation will also be increased if there is a more or less one-to-one relationship between political parties and social forces, that is, if each major group expresses itself politically through a party that exclusively or primarily represents its interests. This effect has been observed for territorial, class, and communal groups. Thus, while competition between parties increases voter turnout (see Chapter Three), voting turnout in competitive elections has also tended to be higher in districts dominated by one party; these districts tend to be socially and economically homogeneous.[40] Lacking competition within the district, the party can more effectively mobilize voters against competition from outside the district.

A party system based on class, or on other distinct social groupings, is also likely to produce higher levels of voter participation. In the United States, with its system of heterogeneous parties composed of a variety of social groups, voting participation reflects status and consequently tends to be relatively low. In Norway, by contrast, status (as measured by education) has no significant relationship to voting participation. Instead, a "class-distinct" party system, operating through networks of related economic and other organizations, produces high turnout and political activity rates among lower-status groups. "In the Norwegian setting, workers and farmers get activated for politics through strong economic organizations dominating distinctive parties of their own: the trade unions in the Labour Party and the farmers' associations in the Agrarian

Party. Family traditions certainly count in the recruitment of 'actives' among workers and farmers, but the decisive influences are organizational: the unions and economic associations create incentives for active participation in party politics and open up opportunities for promotion to positions of trust in the party organizations."[41] This process, leading to high participation rates, has been duplicated in Chile, Argentina, and other developing countries where there is a close correspondence between political party, economic organization, and socio-economic group; it is a common feature of the populist model of development.

More generally, as we have suggested in our discussion of the participatory effects of multifunctional structure, political participation will be increased if all the various human relationships and needs are concentrated in one group and are met through that group. Socialist and Communist parties in Europe have historically aimed to do this by creating "an organized subculture which cuts workers off from the rest of the society." They have attempted

> to organize completely the lives of workers by having them belong to party-controlled unions, live in workers' co-operative housing, belong to party-aligned sports and social clubs, attend cultural and musical activities sponsored by the party or the unions, and read party newspapers and magazines. Children are supposed to grow up belonging to party youth groups.

In Austria, Germany, and France, where working-class parties developed this multifunctional organizational infrastructure, they were often able to achieve voting participation rates of ninety percent or more in working-class districts; in these situations "the usual class differential in voting turnout has been entirely eliminated or even reversed."[42] Similarly, in three out of the four states in India where rural voting turnout exceeded urban turnout, there was a well-developed and active Communist Party.[43]

Alternatives: Individual Mobility versus Group Organization

There are, thus, two distinct channels leading to higher levels of political participation: the mobility channel and the organizational channel. The path of the former leads, in order, from low socio-economic status to individual efforts at mobility; higher socio-economic status; increased subjective feelings of political efficacy, more knowledge about politics, and a clearer perception of the relevance of politics to one's interests; higher levels of political participation; and, incidentally, to organizational involvement. The organizational path, in contrast, leads from low socio-economic status to group (class, communal, or neighborhood) homogeneity and insularity; group conflict with outside forces; increased group consciousness and solidarity; organizational involvement; and, thence, to political participation. These two channels are outlined in Figure 4.2.

Figure 4.2 Channels to Political Participation

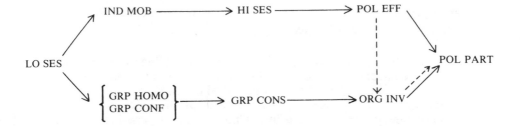

The mobility channel produces political participation at a later date; the organizational channel at an earlier one. Participation that is derived from organization is likely to be partly mobilized and partly autonomous; participation derived from status is likely to be predominantly autonomous. Although organization-derived participation may take the form of electoral action and collective lobbying, it is more likely than status-based participation to involve extra-legal forms of direct action and possibly violence.

Mobility and organization offer contrasting routes to somewhat different results. The one involves individual effort, the other collective action. The route in the one case is from increased material well-being to subjective feelings of political efficacy and thence to political participation; the route in the other case is from subjective feelings of group consciousness to political participation and thence to increased material or symbolic well-being. For the individual, the engine of the one route is education, of the other, organization. For the society, the mobility route means a change in the social status of the individuals but not necessarily in the political participation patterns of groups; the organization route means a change in the political participation patterns of groups, but not necessarily in the social status of individuals.

The polarity of individual mobility and collective action is a familiar one in sociological analysis. In the early 1970s it came to the fore as a simple but useful paradigm for analyzing the social and political choices confronting individuals and groups. Landsberger, for instance, reconceptualized the phenomenon of collective group improvement and applied it to movements appealing to peasants, workers, and other deprived groups. Such movements, he concludes, may confront less repression than they did in the past, but they also have fewer chances of success; their future is gloomy.[44] More generally, Albert Hirschman analyzed responses to the decline in organizations in terms of the choice between "exit" and "voice" and then generalized this analysis to a variety of economic and political situations.[45] Here, as elsewhere in the literature, individual socio-economic mobility and collective political action were seen as alternatives that are practically, if not logically, exclusive.

In due course, individual mobility leads to higher socio-economic status and thus to higher levels of political involvement. In the shorter run, however, an inverse relation may well exist between mobility and participation, and an individual may have to choose between the two. As individual members of ethnic groups in the United States rise significantly above the group norm in socio-economic status, they tend to become less politically participant. Hence, lower income members of ethnic groups often participate more politically than higher-income members of those groups. Similarly, people in different occupational strata from their fathers tend to vote less than people who remain in the same strata.[46] The phenomenon of cross-pressures reducing participation is again at work. In Kenya, as economic opportunities opened up after independence, many who had been politically active abandoned politics and went into business and agriculture; economic success in these roles substituted for the political influence they had exercised earlier and, in some measure, was associated with the firm rejection of efforts to involve them in politics. On the other hand, for those who are upwardly mobile into upper-middle-class or upper-class positions, mobility does not mean, and often cannot mean, a complete renunciation of political activity. In the province of Izmir in Turkey, for instance, sixty-three percent of the local leaders of the more conservative Justice party were upwardly mobile, in the sense that they had higher status occupations than their fathers, while sixty-three percent of the reformist Republican party leaders and eighty-one percent of the radical Turkish Labor party leaders were not upwardly mobile, and, indeed, eleven percent of the latter were downwardly mobile.[47] In general, someone in the middle class, or higher, will already be politically participant as a result of his status; hence, he is more likely to combine further upward mobility with more political participation than is a lower-income person. The latter often lack both mobility and participation and must make a choice between the two. The well-off, in short, may be able to eat their cake and have it too; the poor cannot.

The situation confronting lower income groups has a paradoxical logic, which has been well summed up by Lipset: "the more open the class structure of any society, the more politically apathetic its working class should be; and, conversely, the more rigidly stratified a society, the more likely that its lower classes will develop their own strong form of political activity."[48] In the United States, where class lines have been less rigid and the perceived opportunities for mobility into the middle class have been more extensive, working-class political organizations have been weak, and working-class political participation has been low. A contrasting rigidity, common in Europe in terms of economic class, has been notably present in the United States in terms of race. With limited opportunities for socio-economic mobility, American blacks, particularly lower-status ones, played little role in politics for decades. They identified themselves as being largely outside the systems of both economic mobility and political participation. In the 1950s and 1960s, however, limited improvements in education and employment, plus increased urbanization, combined with the heightened political consciousness and activity of middle-class blacks (and whites on behalf of blacks) to produce a dramatic change in the participation patterns of lower-status blacks. They became more likely to vote, to join organizations, and to engage in political activity, in general, than whites of comparable socio-economic status.[49] Racial barriers thus produced patterns of political activity and levels of political participation among American blacks comparable to those that class barriers produced among European workers.

The inverse relationship with political participation holds for horizontal as well as vertical mobility. In other words, moving one's residence (and perhaps job) may be an alternative to staying put and organizing collectively, just as socio-economic upward mobility may be an alternative to lower-class political organization. Three patterns of response were found among residents of a medium-sized American city who perceived the existence of neighborhood problems. High-status whites, reflecting undoubtedly the efficacy induced by status, tended to respond both by taking political action to correct the problem and also, to a lesser degree, by moving away from the area. Low-status whites, on the other hand, lacking both the personal qualities and the group organization for political action, overwhelmingly preferred exit to voice and preferred to move away from the neighborhood. In contrast, blacks, both low and high status, recognizing the realities of residential segregation by race, overwhelmingly rejected the exit option and instead indicated a strong preference for political action or some combination of exit and voice. The differences in the responses of low-status whites and blacks were, in this respect, quite striking.:[50]

| | Low educated urban | |
Response type	Whites	Blacks
Exit only	40.0%	14.3%
Voice only	13.3	35.7
Exit and voice	13.3	28.6
Neither	33.3	21.4

These figures demonstrate again that low-status blacks tend to be more politically participant than low-status whites.

Comparable options of exit or voice are open to peasants in developing countries, but they are weighted somewhat differently. The peasant may be confronted with deteriorating economic conditions, as a result of changes in the man/land ratio stemming from demographic growth, and with increased inequalities in land ownership, stemming from modernization. In such circumstances, he can find little opportunity for vertical socio-economic mobility within the rural sector. Even when his material conditions in the countryside do not deteriorate, the peasant is likely to be influenced by the appeals of urban life-styles—as a result of radio, highway travel, elementary education, and reports from earlier urban migrants—and to develop aspirations that go beyond his current and prospective way of life. But again, the opportunities for rural vertical mobility are few. The alternatives to the status quo, consequently, are usually either collective political and economic action to better conditions in the countryside, or migration from the countryside to the town or city. The latter, horizontal mobility, almost always involves an improvement in socio-economic status. In Turkey, for instance, migrants in urban squatter settlements typically own their own homes, have three to four times the average rural income, and overwhelmingly express the view that they are better off in the city and do not wish to return to their villages.[51] Collective action, on the other hand, means the formation of syndicates that will bargain with landlords over rents, wages, and services, or that will operate through political means or direct action (and possibly violence) to bring about land reform and a more equitable distribution of land ownership.

Scattered evidence suggests not only that migration and collective action are alternative courses for the individual peasant, but also that they are not often found in the same area at the same time. In Italy, for instance, before World War I, peasants in the central provinces responded to economic hardship by organizing syndicates, conducting strikes, and generally engaging in collective militant activity. There was little out-migration from this area, except when the government suppressed strikes. In the Italian Deep South, on the other hand, with equal or worse poverty, there was no collective action by the peasants, but instead high rates of out-migration.[52] During the 1930s and 1940s in South Vietnam, the economic conditions of the peasantry deteriorated seriously; migration into the cities was not, however, substantial, and social movements—the Cao Dai, Hoa Hao, and Communist party—developed strength in the countryside. More generally, Powell has shown that where the commercialization of agriculture and the politicization of the peasantry occur before substantial urban migration, the results are usually agrarian reform or agrarian revolution. Where commercialization and politicization occur after substantial urbanization, they have little impact.[53] In general, once the processes of socio-economic change have begun in the countryside, the level of peasant political participation in rural areas varies inversely with the rate of peasant out-migration from those areas.

To the extent that this relationship holds true, the next question is: What factors influence or determine the choice of exit vs. voice, mobility vs. participation? In general, an exit propensity seems to prevail among low-status individuals; confronted with a socio-economic challenge, they prefer to respond by individual mobility, horizontal or vertical, rather than by collective political action. Their response is entirely rational: in general, the expected benefits of mobility are higher, and the costs lower, than those of political action.

The benefits low-status people seek are usually enhanced economic well-being and social status. The most direct route to these goals is obviously upward socio-economic mobility. The costs of vertical mobility may include harder work and perhaps a degree of emotional tension. The successful climber may also experience the psychological pains of status incongruency. The psychic costs, however, are seldom anticipated, and, for the ambitious, the additional work is an acceptable price for progress. But for most low-status rural workers, of course, the objective facts of social structure and economic inequality make vertical mobility an extremely remote possibility.

The expected benefits of horizontal mobility—that is, migration— are also fairly direct. Migration is usually a means to the end of enhanced economic well-being: surveys of migrants in dozens of cities of the developing world show that the major motive for migration is improved economic opportunity. Where conditions at home are bad or deteriorating, of course, migration also offers the direct and immediate benefit of escape from these conditions. And for many cityward migrants, moving also offers subsidiary benefits of variety, excitement, and freedom from stultifying rural or small-town social controls.

Horizontal mobility is usually more available than vertical mobility, but it also usually entails higher costs. Among the most obvious and concrete are separation from family and friends, the monetary costs of

No Easy Choice

moving, the risk of not finding work in the new place, and the discomfort of living in an unfamiliar social setting and sometimes in an alien climate and ethnic milieu. These costs are reduced, however, for many migrants who have relatives and friends already established at their destination. Thus although they must leave some family members they soon join others; the risks of settling are reduced, and the psychic costs of moving are lowered because of the familiarity of the process. In some parts of the world, the migrant also has the option of returning home again if the expected benefits of moving fail to materialize.

In contrast to both vertical and horizontal mobility, the option of "voice," or collective political action, usually offers lower benefits and higher costs. Unlike both forms of mobility, political participation is almost never seen as beneficial in and of itself. And as a means of enhancing welfare or status, its benefits are chancy, deferred in time, and often unpredictable in incidence. On the costs side, collective political action involves all of the difficulties of any collective endeavor: overcoming apathy, co-ordinating activity, assigning functions, exercising leadership. It also often costs money. Political action by peasants, if it is to be effective, normally requires the collaborative efforts of outside groups, who may or may not be forthcoming or reliable. Finally, political action often entails the risk of repression by landlords, employers, or the state. All of these costs loom larger for the poor and uneducated than for the affluent.

Obviously, few people weigh the costs and benefits of exit versus voice in an orderly and explicit fashion. Yet their choices do reflect the rationale outlined above. The exit propensity of low-status individuals is likely to be counterbalanced only where the costs of mobility are unusually high or mobility is entirely blocked, or if the costs of political action are greatly reduced or its expected benefits are higher and more certain than normal.

Low-caste groups in India, for example, have traditionally faced immense obstacles to socio-economic mobility. Migration might slightly relax, but could not erase, these obstacles. On the other hand, among some of the low-caste groups, solidarity and a substantial degree of traditional organization facilitated (reduced the costs of) political organization. From the late nineteenth century on (and earlier, in some instances), such groups have used direct collective action, both political and nonpolitical, to seek improvements in their welfare and status. To take a different example, blacks in the southern United States, faced with apparently insurmountable obstacles to both upward mobility and political action, migrated north in large numbers during and after World War II. Once in the North, however, their efforts to improve their welfare further, specifically in housing, neighborhood services, and schooling, by migrating to affluent parts of the cities or to the suburbs, have been blocked. In itself, this did not automatically prompt a turn to political action, but as leadership, resources, and the self-image of the black community strengthened in the 1950s and 1960s, political action to improve inner-city conditions became much more common. In the absence of obstacles to moving out of the city, however, it seems likely that many blacks would have preferred exit to voice, as did most poor whites confronted with deteriorating inner-city conditions. Similarly, rural-to-urban migration may often be reduced or blocked entirely by the existence of different ethnic groups in the city and countryside. This was, at least in part, why Vietnamese peasants in the 1930s and 1940s were slow to move into cities dominated by the French and Chinese. In other instances, of course, vertical mobility will be blocked by ethnic, linguistic, or religious lines that reinforce class cleavages.

In most instances, it would appear that some form of mobility blockage is critical in inducing a choice of voice over exit. But apparently this need not always be the case. MacDonald, for instance, explains the differences between peasant responses in central and southern Italy by the differences in land tenure. In central Italy, land ownership was very unequal; society was polarized between a small number of large landowners and a large number of tenants and laborers; the peasants were, as a result, brought together into a collective class consciousness. In the Italian Deep South, on the other hand, landowning was fragmented, and there were few large estates; consequently, there was no one against whom the peasants could organize. In the absence of this incentive to organization, they instead resorted to migration. In MacDonald's words:

> The key to the labour movement among the cultivators in the Centre and Apulia lies in their class structure. The very unequal distribution systems of the Centre and Apulia, with their discrete classes, provided a structure within which a "class-struggle" could take place. . . .

The economic structure of the Deep South did not provide a context appropriate to labour militancy. The cultivators were placed in a competitive position with each other, and there was not a clear-cut division separating upper and lower class as in the Centre and Apulia. Economic responsibility and enterprise were passed to the individual cultivator and his family. Consequently the cultivators of the Deep South turned to migration instead of the socialist movement.[54]

Given the propensity to exit and the apparent absence of major obstacles to migration, why did the peasants of central Italy choose the usually more difficult and uncertain course of collective political action? Two factors would appear to be most important. First, the economic relationships in central Italy, with a large number of workers employed on a small number of estates, encouraged homogeneity on the part of the workers and conflict between workers and owners. Under these conditions, as we have suggested, group consciousness crystallizes and collective organization is likely to emerge. In southern Italy, the minifundia peasants were isolated from each other, often competed with each other, and lacked any clearly identifiable common enemy. Second, collective political action requires not only a sense of misery but also a sense of outrage and injustice. The peasants of southern Italy may have perceived their situation as miserable, but it would be difficult for them to perceive it as unjust. But where, as in central Italy, the economic and social structure make exploitation, in Weber's phrase, "transparent," then anger is likely to be added to misery. And this outrage or sense of injustice is more likely to result in political action. The sense of injustice is all the more likely to manifest itself: (a) if the current exploitation represents a change from an earlier pattern, for instance, if the rents charged by absentee landlords increase, or (b) if education, the media, or new—and most likely external—leadership encourage the poor to redefine their existing situation as one of exploitation. Thus, favorable "objective" conditions encouraging intragroup homogeneity and extragroup conflict, plus a sense of moral indignation, may lead to collective political action even if exit is also readily available.

What we have referred to as the exit propensity of low-income groups obviously poses dilemmas for those interested in expanding political participation in general and participation by low-income groups in particular. In the absence of counter-efforts, such groups, when given a choice, will tend to opt for individual socio-economic mobility rather than for collective political participation. In due course, this should, of course, lead to higher levels of status-derived, autonomous political participation. But it can be argued that such participation may be an unrealistic dream, and that once delayed in the development process, political participation may be indefinitely postponed. Just as the immediate beneficiaries of economic growth in society may act to impede subsequent movement toward economic equity, so also those who are politically participant in early phases may act to resist broader sharing in the political process. Bureaucratic middle-class groups, for instance, like civil servants and army officers, may oppose the extension of participation to upwardly-mobile entrepreneurial and professional middle-class groups.

The alternative to this potentiality is to take active measures in the early phases of development to promote political participation as an autonomous and important goal. This could, logically, mean sharpening the cleavages in society, hardening the social structure, encouraging residential segregation, restricting horizontal and vertical mobility, intensifying group consciousness, and stimulating lower-class organizations. However unattractive these measures might appear to the well-meaning liberal, some combination of them would, in all probability, be the most expeditious way of rapidly increasing political participation in most developing countries. Some of these strategies are, indeed, precisely the ways in which the leadership of communist parties attempt to mobilize political participation to support their goals of fundamentally restructuring the economy and society. There is, in some measure, a trade-off between social harmony and political participation. This point is made not to recommend one course or another, nor to suggest that, in fact, any society will pursue the mobility channel or the organizational channel to the total exclusion of the other. It is made, rather, to underline the extent to which the expansion of political participation itself has implications for other values often thought to be desirable, and to clarify the choices that individuals, groups, and governments may have to make among these values.

Sequences: Individual Mobility and Group Organization

At any given time, people unwilling to accept their current situation confront two alternative routes to improvement: individual mobility or collective organization. The opportunity and the need to make these choices recur in the lives of individuals, families, and groups. The choices made at these points determine the different sequences of social and political change that predominate in different societies. For the particular actor, they may also produce recurring patterns of preference for mobility or organization, or, sometimes, a pattern of alternation between these routes to progress. While it is often difficult, and at times impossible, to pursue both channels simultaneously, it is possible and often necessary to pursue them sequentially. In the history of individuals and groups, mobility and organization may interact with each other in almost dialectical fashion. Successful mobility means status improvement and enhanced potential for organizational involvement and autonomous political action. Lack of success in mobility may lead to collective political efforts or, if these have already been exhausted, to resignation. In addition, successful collective action will create the basis for increased welfare and status, and increased status normally leads to political consciousness and the potential for political action. Both socio-economic mobility and collective political involvement may, in short, be discontinuous processes. Just as societies may alternate between the technocratic and the populist models, so also may individuals alternate between individual mobility and collective action.

Differences in mobility opportunities and in group contexts permit a great variety of choice sequences. But the basic processes of urbanization and industrialization produce certain sequences more frequently than others, both in the lives of individuals and families, and for societies as a whole. The possibility of group-based political action, derived from intergroup conflict and intragroup homogeneity, arises only at certain points in the individual's encounter with social and economic change. In the absence of communal divisions within society, there is, in the evolution of society and of the individual, a more or less natural sequence of three opportunities for group-based political action, based respectively on the group consciousness of the peasant, the migrant, and the worker. In the first and third opportunities, the consciousness is class consciousness; in the second, migrants may take group action on the basis of neighborhood solidarity or as a reflection of continuing identification with their places of origin. But the pattern of choice for migrants is more variable and less clear-cut than the pattern for peasants or for workers who have become fairly well-integrated into the urban industrial economy. Each of these three bases for organizing involves different challenges to the existing order and different demands against that order; in general, the challenge tends to decline sequentially from one opportunity to the next. In a sense, a choice has to be made in each case between group action and some form of individual mobility. If collective action is chosen and is successful, it has the effect of improving the status of the individual. Even when chosen, however, collective action may not be sustained for long. Status, once achieved, is normally retained for a lifetime and is often transmitted to the next generation; consequently, it provides a relatively stable and sustained basis for political participation. Group action, on the other hand, depends on a favorable context of homogeneity and conflict; that context can shift rapidly as a result of socio-economic changes in the society.

The first choice in the developmental sequence is made by the peasant. In some areas, population pressure, technological change, or shifts in land tenure may leave segments of the rural population worse off than in the past. Elsewhere, rural conditions may be static or may even improve slightly, while the gap between rural and urban opportunities is widening. The peasant then confronts several alternatives. He may choose a definitive move to the city, committing himself to a very different style of life. Where rural social and economic conditions permit or encourage return migration, as in much of Africa and South and Southeast Asia, he may choose to go to the city on a temporary basis, for a few months or years, earning enough to make ends meet or to support a more comfortable rural life, but retaining his commitment to the countryside.[55] Or the peasant may decide to stay in the countryside and take collective action to improve his situation. While permanent migration is a clear alternative to collective action, temporary migration and rural political organization are not necessarily mutually exclusive, and, indeed, the former may encourage the latter under some circumstances.

For reasons outlined above, the peasant is more likely to choose migration than politics. If there are, however, mobility blockages, and if conditions (particularly in the form of potential urban allies) favor peasant organization, the path of collective action may be chosen. This normally involves a significant challenge to the existing social order; the targets of peasant political action are local landlords and officials, and the goals of that action are usually a drastic revamping of land tenure arrangements. In the absence of support from a significant element of the urban population—the military, intelligentsia, bureaucracy, or autocratic ruler—peasant collective action has great difficulty in achieving its goal. The failure of group action is likely to have a major deterrent effect on the likelihood of subsequent political organization, and to increase the probability of migration as a future response. The success of collective peasant action converts tenants and landless laborers into landowners and reduces overall inequality in land ownership. As few other government policies do, land reform thus contributes both to status elevation and status equality, and hence provides a continuing basis for status-derived political participation. For land reform to be effective, peasant organizations must participate on a sustained basis in the administration of the program. This program participation imperative is met in part by the political efficacy the peasants derive from status improvements and in part by the organizational involvement derived from peasant group consciousness.

Many peasants, however, choose mobility over organization and migrate to the cities. The patterns of migration vary greatly, of course, from country to country and from region to region. They may take the form of migration to provincial towns or metropolitan centers, of step migration, of back-and-forth migration, of individual migration or family migration. Both the pattern of migration and the specific urban context affect the probability that the migrant will be drawn into collective action once he is in the city.

Where many migrants are not committed to permanent urban residence, continued loyalty to the place of origin, coupled with heightened group consciousness and political sophistication fostered by the urban setting, may encourage home-place (provincial, tribal, home-town) associations. Such associations are usually multi-functional, and their activities often include efforts to lobby for assistance to the place of origin. Thus, temporary horizontal mobility may lay the basis for collective action, among at least some migrants.[56]

Where permanent migration is the rule, individual and family efforts to improve status and livelihood normally absorb most migrants' full energies. As will be discussed in the next chapter, neither the entry occupations that are common among migrants and the urban poor generally, nor many of their residential arrangements, provide a basis for political organization. Some migrants, however, do go directly or eventually into squatter settlements. And such settlements can furnish the context and need for collective political action.

The origin of the settlement often plays a critical role in shaping its members' political participation during at least the earlier phases of its existence. As Cornelius has observed,

> a land invasion—whether organized or spontaneously initiated—may be a crucial unifying and politicizing experience for community residents. This is especially true if the initial seizure of land is followed by repeated attempts at eviction by the government or private landowners. . . . The illegal origins of squatter settlements and unauthorized subdivisions also define their relationships with political and governmental agencies for many years to come, and create a major community problem—insecurity of land tenure—on which cooperative political activity among the residents may focus. . . . The old social-psychological maxim of "out-group hostility, in-group solidarity" appears to have considerable relevance here.[57]

Organized land invasions, while frequent in certain Latin American nations (particularly Peru, but also Chile, Colombia, Mexico, and Venezuela), are rare or nonexistent in other regions. The great bulk of squatter settlements are formed according to the "dribble-in" pattern, where a few squatters build pioneer huts and are gradually or rapidly joined by others, often relatives and friends at first, until the available space is filled. But even in such noninvasion settlements, mutual co-operation and political activity may be high. In a manner somewhat reminiscent of what supposedly happened in pioneer settlements on the American frontier, between forty and sixty-five percent of *gecekondu* residents in two Turkish cities received help from or exchanged help with fellow residents. The associational ties of these migrants were also much more extensive than those of the rural population. About one-third of the household heads in the *gecekondu* areas of Ankara, for instance, belonged to formal associations, and the most important of these groups, the community associations or *derneks*, played a key role in relating individuals to the broader political system and in defending the interests of the settlement to the government authorities.[58]

Thus, the peasant who resorts to horizontal mobility, rather than to collective peasant (i.e., class-based) organization in the countryside, may sometimes engage in collective migrant (i.e., neighborhood-based) organization once in the city. In both instances the stimulus to group organization is usually the perceived need for land and home ownership. Demands for changes in ownership are usually more challenging to the established order than demands for changes in income allocation and, hence, are more likely to generate resistance, on the one side, and group consciousness, on the other. In both cases, the goals are relatively concrete, and their achievement brings an immediate improvement in status.

The degree of challenge and the potential for revolutionary activity is, however, considerably less in the city than in the countryside. The confrontation in the countryside between owner and tenant, or owner and landless laborer, is, both in fact and in perception, a zero-sum situation. In the city, the land occupied by migrants for squatter settlements is more likely to be either public land or privately owned but unused or low-value land. It is not normally land currently used for income-producing purposes. In addition, the demands for land reform in rural areas usually involve a restructuring of relationships throughout much of the countryside, while the demands of urban squatters can be met on a piecemeal basis, neighborhood by neighborhood or even individual by individual. Once the migrants establish their community, moreover, they are likely to follow a relatively conservative political course. Migrants eschew involvement in political protests because they see little to be gained by such activity. Except in the case of land invasions, the migrant normally prefers to use conventional forms of political demand-making both because of a "commitment to abiding by the political rules of the game in his new environment" and because of the greater efficacy of such methods.[59] Among Pakistani cities in the 1960s, for instance, political violence correlated negatively with the number of refugees and persons born outside a city and had no correlation with the growth rate of the urban population.[60]

Where competitive elections are held, migrants, with some exceptions, such as the 1970 vote for ANAPO in Colombia, tend to vote for more conservative parties and to be less opposition-oriented than more prosperous groups in a city. In Turkey, until 1973, the more conservative

Justice party got a disproportionate share of the *gecekondu* vote, presumably because of the substantial social mobility demonstrated by *gecekondu* residents and because the Justice party dominated many municipal governments and was, therefore, in a position to reward or to punish neighborhoods, a crucial possibility to neighborhoods clearly in need of improvements in municipal services. In Latin America, migrants "have tended toward political conservatism, in the sense of not favoring drastic alterations in the socio-political status quo." This conservatism is "rooted in a deeply felt need to preserve the modest but nonetheless significant gains in income level, living conditions, and property conditions, and property accumulation (particularly in the form of a homesite on the urban periphery) which he has achieved." Also relevant are the migrant's view of "the opportunity structure in urban areas as being relatively open," and his continued "belief in the potential for future social and economic betterment for himself and particularly for his children within the ongoing system."[61] Thus, there would appear to be an overall positive relationship between individual socio-economic mobility (in this case in the form of urban migration) and a propensity toward more conservative and intrasystem, as distinguished from extrasystem, forms of political action.

Consistent with this tendency toward political moderation and an emphasis on individual mobility, even that fraction of migrants who become involved in collective action through squatter associations do not continue this involvement very long. The highest priority goal among squatters is governmental recognition of land titles, or at least some indication of official acquiescence in their de facto tenure. Once this goal is achieved, the need for urban services provides additional stimuli of generally decreasing urgency; next after security of tenure comes water, sewage systems, and electricity. Virtually all residents of the community share an equal interest in these needs. Once they are met, demands will be advanced for facilities such as schools, public markets, health centers, and the like. These, however, are less universal needs and are less likely to be met in timely fashion through collective neighborhood action. And once these "most acute developmental problems are resolved, rates of participation in community improvement associations and all other forms of cooperative political activity tend to decline sharply." Neighborhood-based political action is a means to an end; it will be sustained only if there exists "a set of high-priority, community-related problems which can be addressed *most effectively* through collective political action."[62]

The decline in neighborhood-based political organization is, presumably, accompanied by additional efforts at individual mobility, through self-help action in improving one's home and by increased attention to employment mobility. The status improvements that have been brought about by collective political action provide a base for further efforts at individual mobility. In this respect, the children of migrants seem to be more highly oriented toward mobility, and away from politics, than their parents. As mobility opportunities open up, organization loses its appeal and political participation, based on organizational involvement, declines.

This pattern, which is common among the population of squatter settlements, can also be seen in similar circumstances on a different scale. The creation of a nation-state, like that of a squatter settlement, involves high levels of political participation by many groups in the population. If opportunities for individual socio-economic mobility exist after the state is established, there may well be a shift from the one to the other. In Kenya, for instance, upwardly mobile individuals participated in the nationalist movement, used it to achieve access to economic advantages and opportunities, and then shifted out of politics to pursue commercial and business careers. In Kenya, "active membership in KANU declined in many parts of the country after independence and . . . many people of talent and energy went elsewhere to pursue their interests." This shift was "as much or more a function of opportunities opening up in commercial and agricultural spheres as it was unhappiness with KANU."[63]

In an early phase of social science urban research, it was frequently predicted that urban migrants themselves would be an explosive political force in the cities. This has definitely turned out not to be the case, as migrants have found it worthwhile to pursue fairly specific material goals within the existing political system. It was then argued, in a second phase of urban research, that while the modest aspirations and commensurate progress of the migrants might make them a relatively quiescent and even conservative political force, their children would be very different.

Growing up in the city, they would have much higher aspirations and if these were not met, as inevitably they would not be in large part, the slums of the Third World would be "swept by social violence, as the children of the city demand the rewards of the city."[64]

While the historical evidence from Europe and North America lends considerable support to this "second generation" hypothesis, it has not as yet been confirmed by evidence from the contemporary Third World cities. Indeed, in some respects, the slight evidence available tends to call the theory into question or to demand its qualification. Cornelius's work on Mexico City shows the second generation to have higher levels of political knowledge and awareness than the first, that is, to have more of the attitudes that normally go with political participation than their parents had. But they also "participate in politics significantly less than their parents." In addition, they "do not exhibit significantly more negative evaluations of the political system than their parents, nor are they significantly more dissatisfied with the government's performance, frustrated with their personal situation, ideologically radicalized, or politically involved."[65] This sustained acquiescence, plus the decline in political participation, is explained by the failure of the second generation to undergo the political learning experiences, such as the land invasions and other confrontations, that developed group political consciousness among their parents. The second generation does in fact have a significantly weaker disposition than the first to engage in cooperative behavior. Its members want to get ahead individually, not to work together collectively. They are likely to "be more concerned with the requisites for individual social and economic mobility than with community needs and problems which can be addressed more appropriately through collective political action." Hence, to the extent that they do make political demands, these demands "will have a particularistic rather than a collective referent."[66]

A concern with individual mobility also predominates among Turkish *gecekondu* dwellers, particularly in terms of their aspirations for their children. Evidence from two cities shows that a majority of *gecekondu* dwellers aspire to middle-class occupations and to middle-class living standards, rather than to some collective improvement within the working classes. The migrants want educational opportunities for their children and believe that their children can reach high positions if they have the ability. The prevailing myth is one of middle-class mobility, not working-class consciousness. On the one hand, as Özbuden points out, this means that the migrants have clearly imbibed "modern," urban, middle-class values. On the other hand, such values clearly "present serious obstacles to the efforts of achieving collective mobility for the urban poor by way of class-oriented political action."[67]

The critical test of the second generation hypothesis is likely to be whether the second and third generation migrants are indeed able to realize their job-mobility aspirations. If, as seems highly probable in Mexico, Turkey, and other developing countries, a substantial portion of them are not able to achieve the vertical mobility they aspire to, then the stage will be set for a new turn to collective political action: "Individualistic political attitudes may give way to more collective political orientations, and a radicalization of the urban poor may eventually take place."[68] Their political action, however, is not likely to take the form of a slum revolt. Conceivably, it could manifest itself as employment-oriented or job-based economic and political action through trade unions and political parties affiliated with trade unions. The obstacles to effective union organization, however, are also great, since so much employment is in relatively small firms, and a major gap exists between such employees and the small number of relatively affluent workers in the large firms. Workers in small enterprises, who face unemployment, as well as small entrepreneurs themselves, who face business failure, are potential recruits for populist or right-wing parties attacking the political establishment of the center. Whatever its specific manifestation, mobility blockage, in the form of a shortage of middle-class employment opportunities, could give rise to class-consciousness, organization, and political participation. This participation would also derive strength from the status improvement, such as better education and home security, that had been achieved following the earlier generation's migration to the city.

Conclusion

In summary, the opportunities and inducements open to the low-status individual involved in socio-economic change seem to suggest a model of alternating mobility and organization. A common sequence, particularly for Latin America, is as follows: *first*, mobility in the form of urban migration; *second*, for those migrants who become squatters —organization in the form of neighborhood associations to secure home ownership and urban services; *third*, mobility in the form of the search for more skilled and higher paying jobs; *fourth*, possibly—if middle-class mobility is blocked—organization in the form of working-class unions, parties partially oriented to working-class problems, or populist movements. Where many migrants are temporary, as in Africa and parts of Asia, different patterns will appear, particularly in the first and second phases. And where politics is organized largely on communal lines, issues and loyalties are likely to cut across both urban-rural boundaries and class differences, so that the categories of peasant, migrant, and worker are less likely to provide a basis for collective political action, although there may still be a salient interplay of opportunities for mobility and collective organization.

For the individual, political participation in general, and organization-derived participation in particular, is usually a means to an end, and that end is usually some form of improvement in his social and economic status. The individual also generally sees his own efforts at socio-economic mobility—through migration, education, or job betterment —as more effective, more direct, less costly, and less risky routes to his goal than collective political action. Only if mobility is blocked does he turn to organization. His involvement in politics usually occurs when he sees no alternative to it. In due course, the effects of mobility and organization alter the distribution of statuses in society and thus provide the basis for higher levels of political efficacy and higher levels of autonomous political participation. In this sense, high levels of status-derived political participation testify to the levels of modernity of the society. High levels of organization-derived participation testify to the blockages that hinder individual mobility.

The opportunities, incentives, and costs associated with collective organization and individual mobility vary tremendously from one type of political and social system to another. Societies at relatively lower levels of socio-economic modernization and political participation can be analysed in terms of the bourgeois and autocratic models of development.

(See Chapter Two.) In a society approximating the bourgeois model, the prevailing conditions greatly favor migration and mobility over collective political action in both the urban and rural sectors. In the countryside, substantial landowners would presumably be engaged in the commercialization of agriculture—extending their holdings, rationalizing their operations, greatly expanding their capital investment, improving their efficiency through fertilizer, irrigation, and modern techniques—all to the end of turning the agricultural unit (estate, plantation, or medium-sized farm) into a highly profitable enterprise. One consequence of this trend is an increase in the likelihood that there will be a surplus of labor in the countryside and hence an enhancement of the appeals of urban migration. In the urban sector of the bourgeois model, the expansion of political participation to the middle class normally manifests itself in the formation of parties based on ideology and personality, rather than parties having deep roots in, and articulating the interests of, particular social classes. In the absence of a politically participant working class, middle-class participation is likely to be fragmented. The stress on the development of a capitalist economy, on the other hand, appears to create more opportunities for individual advancement. By its very nature, the bourgeois system favors personalistic relations, clientelism, and individual mobility.

In the autocratic system, the government prohibits organized political participation by the urban middle class; meanwhile, the emphasis on economic growth and the receptivity to foreign investment tend to open up continuing opportunities for socio-economic mobility. If the government pursues a laissez-faire policy in the countryside, the process of development will not differ significantly from that which occurs under the bourgeois model, and strong incentives will appear favoring urban migration. If, on the other hand, the political elite uses governmental power to force through a land reform in the countryside, the stimulus to urban migration will be reduced. If the reform is to be meaningful and permanent, its beneficiaries and prospective beneficiaries will have to be brought together in a class-based organization. In the longer run, this organization (or congeries of organizations) can become the political vehicle through which the peasant-beneficiaries of the reform defend their interests and advance new claims on government.

At higher levels of socio-economic modernization, the society is often faced by a choice between the technocratic and populist models, or some combination of the two. In a technocratic system, working class political organization is prohibited, middle-class organization is not encouraged, and the stress in both urban and rural sectors is on the goal of economic growth and, hence, the multiplication of opportunities for individual mobility. In a populist system, on the other hand, just the reverse is the case: economic growth is not an overriding goal and opportunities for individual mobility may well decrease in number. The emphasis, instead, is on social justice and equity; in the pursuit of this goal, the organization of the urban and rural working classes receives high priority. If middle-class organization is permitted, it also intensifies, in an effort to counter the claims advanced by the working class organizations.

Among these four models of developmental systems, the populist model is the only one that is clearly structured to encourage collective organization over individual mobility. The others, with the exception of the potentially favorable impact of the autocratic system on peasant organization, all give first priority to multiplying the opportunities for individual mobility, horizontal and vertical. There is, thus, apparently an "exit propensity" for societies, as well as individuals, and the propensity of the latter is a function of the way in which the larger society and its leaders structure the available choices.

Political
Participation
by the Poor

The last two chapters have explored how aspects of modernization affect political participation, both in the society as a whole and at the level of the individual citizen. This chapter considers patterns of political participation at the intermediate level of socio-economic groups. More specifically, it examines the processes through which initially inactive groups become politically participant and break, or are drawn, into the national political arena.

In some ways, these processes echo the experience of the industrialized nations of Western Europe and North America during the nineteenth and early twentieth centuries. A major—perhaps the dominant—theme of their political history during this period was the uneven but continuous spread of participation to middle-class groups, the working classes, women, and specific disadvantaged groups, such as blacks in the United States. But the political inheritance and the social and economic characteristics of most of today's modernizing nations differ in important ways from Western Europe and North America in the nineteenth century, and to a lesser extent from Eastern Europe in the first third of the twentieth century. Therefore, the patterns and processes through which less privileged groups became participant in contemporary Asia, Africa, and Latin America diverge from the patterns of the earlier-developing nations. This divergence is particularly marked in the very poorest groups.

Obstacles to Participation by the Poor

Both the rural and urban poor face major obstacles to participation. By "the poor" we mean, in rural areas, subsistence and sub-subsistence cultivators and agricultural workers. We include those who own, rent, sharecrop, or have access under communal traditions to barely enough land to sustain themselves and their families (subsistence farmers), as well as those with even less land or none at all, who must rely for part or all of their income on wage labor.[1] In urban areas we have in mind those with little or no education or skills, who are employed at insecure, low-paid, and dead-end jobs, most commonly in small-scale manufacturing and service establishments, domestic and custodial service, construction, loading and carrying, or other forms of unskilled day labor. Also included among the urban poor are those who eke out livelihoods by small-scale peddling, salvaging and selling or reworking scrap materials, petty services (shoe-shining, car watching) or small-scale illegal activities (stealing, prostitution, begging, beer-brewing, or the like). Such persons and their families constitute perhaps the bottom forty or fifty percent of the urban income distribution in most developing nations. We do not include most workers with regular jobs in larger-scale modern manufacturing or service firms.[2]

The poor usually take little part in politics because participation often seems irrelevant to their primary concerns, futile, or both. The most pressing problems for many of the poor are jobs, food, and medical aid—for today, tomorrow, or next week. Among the developing nations, only the communist states, and a very few of the more advanced or oil-rich of the non-communist states, provide sizeable programs of welfare or unemployment compensation. Public works programs to ease unemployment are more common, but tend to be sporadic. A larger number of nations do offer free medical service, although facilities are often grossly inadequate. In general, the limited scope of government activity directly relevant to the very poor means that individual contacting of government agencies is irrelevant to many urgent problems. It is still less plausible to take collective action with others among the poor in an effort to influence the government. Instead, the poor turn to their families and friends, priests or other religious leaders, shopkeepers, landlords, schoolteachers, present or past employers, or anyone who is better off and may be in a position to help.

Not only the nature of the poor's most urgent problems, but also their ignorance, may make governmental action seem irrelevant to them. In rural areas especially, most may simply be unaware of national government policies and programs. Even where information is available, they may not realize the connection between their own interests and certain government policies, such as exchange rates or tax incentives that encourage capital-intensive investment.

Both the urban and rural poor, however, may recognize other ways in which local and national government policies and programs do affect their interests Among the more obvious in rural areas are agricultural credit programs, rural roads, irrigation schemes, and schools. In the cities, land titles and public services for squatter areas, schools and clinics, bus fares, and subsidized food prices are a few of the widely recognized ways in which government does, or could, affect the lives of the poor. But even on matters where the government is viewed as relevant, the poor are apt to conclude that individual and collective efforts to exert influence are futile.

There are several reasons for this sense of low efficacy. First, the poor lack resources for effective participation—adequate information, appropriate contacts, money, and often time. Second, in low-income strata, people are often divided by race, tribe, religion, or language; even where the cleavages are not obvious, distinctions may be drawn on the basis of differences in sect, income, status, or place of origin that outsiders can barely perceive. More privileged groups may draw similar distinctions, but they are often better able to cooperate across such lines when joint economic or political interests are at stake. Third, the poor tend to expect requests or pressures on their part, whether individual or collective, to be ignored or refused by the authorities, and these expectations are often justified. Worse, their attempts may provoke governmental repression or prompt reprisals from the private interests threatened by the self-assertion of the poor. Those on the margin of subsistence are particularly vulnerable to threats from employers, landlords, or creditors.

The obstacles to political participation by the poor may take somewhat different forms in rural and urban areas. Some years ago, it was widely assumed that peasant political activity was hindered by deeply ingrained attitudes of fatalism and by deference to social and political superiors. More recently, this assumption has come to be questioned, just as the assumed conservatism towards new techniques of cultivation has been questioned. It is now increasingly recognized that peasant resistance to technical and economic change often reflects objective circumstances—a very narrow margin for risk or share-crop arrangements that reduce the returns of the innovation to the peasant—rather than innate attitudes or sheer force of habit. Similarly, political passivity often reflects the facts of the peasants' lives rather than deference or apathy. In some nations widely dispersed settlement patterns and poor communications hamper political organization. In many areas laborers, tenants, sharecroppers, and smallholders alike depend on one or a few landlords, who are the sole source of wage employment, assistance in emergencies, brokerage with government officials, and other benefits. Thus, the rural poor are often more vulnerable to informal sanctions for maverick political behavior than are their urban counterparts, who have a wider range of alternative sources of employment, credit, emergency assistance, and brokerage.[3]

In urban settings, dependence is less concentrated and personalized, and the urban poor may be better educated and informed than their rural counterparts. But organized political activity remains extremely difficult. Job turnover is high; many, including domestic servants and employees in small manufacturing, repair, or service establishments, work face to face with their employers. Neither of these conditions fosters organization on the basis of shared economic interests. Neighborhood-based organization is an alternative, but many of the urban poor rent rooms or bed-space and move frequently. Moreover, in Africa and parts of South Asia, much of the urban population consists of migrants who plan to return eventually to their home village.[4] Neither renters nor nonpermanent migrants have much incentive to take part in collective political efforts to improve their houses and their neighborhoods. Such efforts are most likely to appear in some of the newer squatter settlements in Latin American, Turkish, Philippine, and other cities, where most migrants are permanent and the settlements comprise mostly families seeking to establish long-term homes and a decent neighborhood. While such settlements house hundreds of thousands of people, in global perspective they represent only a small fraction of the urban poor.

In short, for most of the poor under most conditions, political participation was and is, objectively, a difficult and probably ineffective means of coping with their problems or advancing their interests. Survey findings reflect this: comparatively small proportions of low-income, poorly-educated people are interested in politics, regard politics as relevant to their concerns, or feel able to exert any influence on local or national authorities. Ignorance and strictly attitudinal obstacles—traditional sentiments of deference or fatalism, or a more modern but equally paralyzing "culture of poverty"—may buttress the objective difficulties. But the basic obstacles and lack of incentives are imbedded in the facts of life, and not in the attitudes of low-income groups.

Of course, political participation by the poor is also influenced by the receptivity of already established political groups. At the most elementary level is the legal right to participate. In Brazil and Ecuador, as of the early 1970s, illiterates were still not permitted to vote, and elsewhere they have only recently been enfranchised. Property qualifications are required for participation in some local municipal elections. Beyond legal rights lie questions of institutional and social sanctions and other pressures that encourage or discourage participation. Historically, at each step in the expansion of political participation, those groups already in the political arena (national or local) have found it hard to accept as legitimate the demands of their social "inferiors" or economic dependents, not only for a share in services and benefits provided by the state, but also for a voice in decisions about programs and policies affecting their interests. Certain forms of participation—especially the vote—have been more readily recognized as legitimate than other forms—for example, strikes or demonstrations. In general, the expansion of participation to individuals has been more readily accepted than the expansion of collective participation to previously nonparticipant and unorganized groups. Actually responding to some of the demands of newly participant groups is, of course, still a further step.

In most historical instances, increased politicization and participation by previously inactive groups has forced elite acceptance and a degree of responsiveness. This was the sequence of events in England in the expansion of participation to middle-class groups, and, later, to upper-level working-class strata, in the fight for union recognition in the United States, and in the struggle for female suffrage, to cite only a few examples. In some cases, elite acceptance of at least formal participation preceded widespread participation by group members. For example, until recently, turnout among black voters has been low even in the northern states, although their right to vote was not disputed in those states. Changes in elite attitudes and responsiveness may, then, either lag or lead changes in perceptions and behavior on the part of the newly participant group. The basic point is that they interact. The process of expanding participation cannot be understood by examining the newly participant group in isolation from the broader system.

At the level of abstract political culture and formal laws and institutions, all but the most conservative of today's developing nations are far better prepared to accept, or even promote, widespread political participation than were most European elites during the nineteenth and early twentieth centuries. Despite a few exceptions, universal suffrage is the rule. Most elites give at least lip service to the idea of broad popular participation in governing their countries, although their views differ markedly on the range of issues on which participation is desirable. Those regimes sincerely committed to promoting economic and social development often (though not always) view broadened participation at local levels, and on certain issues, as important stimulants to initiative, efficiency, and honesty. Most regimes, regardless of whether they are dedicated to development or not, feel a certain pressure from international norms to maintain at least the facade of broad popular support. Moreover, the revolutions of the twentieth century have created some awareness of the risks of postponing liberalization too long.

Not only the concept of popular political participation but also a range of participation "technology" is available to the developing nations from the experience of the industrialized world. In England and the United States, in France and the rest of Western Europe, a variety of legal and political institutions, procedures, and techniques have been developed over the past century and a half to facilitate and regulate political organization and the expression of citizens' preferences. More recently the Soviet Union, China, or Yugoslavia offer contrasting models. Many of the former colonies gained independence partly through the efforts of middle-class movements that had some working-class and peasant support. In effect, these nations were born prepared for broad participation, although independence movements often disintegrated after independence. And all modernizing nations, regardless of their colonial experience or the lack of it, can observe and learn from a variety of past experiences with political mobilization in other nations. While elites in early nineteenth century Europe could barely imagine procedures and institutions for mass participation, any more than they could visualize modern production techniques, today's political leaders can choose from, or combine, many patterns.

While political culture and political structure are more open to lower-class participation now than in nineteenth century Europe, most members of elites in Asia, Africa, and Latin America are certainly not eager to give up their traditional privileges, nor are upwardly-mobile middle-class groups prepared to mark time while the poor catch up. Precisely because the political culture is more receptive, the concrete realities of resistance to broadened participation may produce even more bitter conflict than occurred in Europe and North America.

Patterns of Participation by the Poor: An Overview

A random sample of the cases where segments of the urban or rural poor have sought to influence governmental decisions, on their own or others' initiative, would span a great variety of specific forms and combinations. No comparative or theoretical analysis can pretend to explain or predict these variations in detail. We can, however, suggest some of the major channels for bringing rural and urban poor into the national political arena, the issues and forms of participation characteristic of each channel, and some of the conditions under which each is likely to be important.

Table 5.1 is a schematic classification of several major patterns of participation by low-income groups. The patterns differ in scale, source of leadership, goals, and in the probable duration and characteristics of action. The second pattern, particularized contacting, is clearcut and readily distinguished from the rest. The remainder are conceptually distinct, although the boundaries between them are sometimes blurred in reality. In particular countries, specific parties, movements, or associations may combine characteristics of two or more of the patterns. Nor does a single pattern describe the political situation in an entire country; in any one country, several or all of the patterns may be present. Nor is the classification necessarily exhaustive; there may be instances of low-income participation that do not fit any of the categories.

Table 5.1 Patterns of Low-Income Political Participation

Pattern	Leadership	Leaders' Goals	Goals of Low-Income Participants	Scale and Duration of Action	Form(s) of Action
1. Mobilized participation.	Tribal chief or clan elder; patron (landlord or other); ward boss or cacique.	Protect or improve own political and economic interests.	Please, placate, or win favors from leader, patron, or machine.	Usually small or medium-scale, episodic.	Usually voting. Sometimes campaigning, demonstrations.
2. Particularized contacting.	Not applicable.	Not applicable.	Solve specific individual problem.	Individual only, episodic.	Petitioning, bribery.
3. Small-scale specific interest group.	Usually local, low or low-middle income influentials. Sometimes outside charitable or political organizers.	Solve own and community problems, gain prestige, sometimes gain material benefits.	Improve own and community circumstances, usually through better facilities. (Well, access road, electricity).	Small-scale, single shot.	Collective self-help, petitioning, publicity. Occasional block-vote bargaining.
4. Cross-class (ethnic, nationalist) party or movement.	Elite and/or middle-class politicians.	Defend or promote nationalist, regional, or ethnic, economic or symbolic interests.	Same as leaders'.	Often large-scale, and sometimes sustained.	All collective forms. Issues are emotional, therefore some tendency to violence.
5. Large-scale lower-class oriented.	Elite and/or middle-class politicians.	Ideological commitment and/or response to political competition.	Improve own and peers' material circumstances.	Medium or large-scale, sometimes sustained.	All collective forms. Voting, campaigning, demonstrations most common.

The patterns described in Table 5.1 are not unique to the poor, but poor people are more likely to participate through these than through other patterns, because each of these patterns has a built-in mechanism for overcoming the obstacles that confront the poor. More specifically, each of these patterns incorporates a different means for heightening relevance and strengthening potential participants' feelings of efficacy. The three patterns that involve collective action also incorporate means for overcoming barriers to cooperation and trust.

The mobilized pattern does not really overcome obstacles to political participation; it finesses them by redefining the purpose of the action. If the poor participant views his vote, campaign activity, or other action as a means to mollify a feared leader or to express his loyalty and respect for a traditional chief, religious leader, or needed patron, he need not even consider whether the government is relevant to his needs, or whether his action is likely to affect it. His action serves its purpose immediately and directly, regardless of its impact on the government. Since he acts as an individual, without regard to his peers, the issue of trust and cooperation with those peers does not arise.

Particularized contacting assures relevance and efficacy by focusing on very specific and selected goals, of types known to be provided by the government. The link between participation (contacting) and results is direct and immediate. Similarly, small-scale interest groups, such as neighborhood associations, usually form around specific, narrow, and often single-shot issues that are perceived as important by all in the group and are susceptible to solution through government action. The capacity for collective action is promoted, though far from guaranteed, by the small scale and stability of the group. But the same features that permit many poor people to participate through this pattern, at one time or another, also limit its durability and scope.

Poor people are often brought into politics on the basis of issues or loyalties that cut across class lines. For example, concern over inflation involves the poor jointly with organized labor and lower middle class groups. Ethnic cleavages in many nations cut across, rather than coinciding with, class stratification. For the poor, such issues or loyalties ease the problems of relevance and efficacy by joining their own interests with those of better-placed and more influential groups. The poor participants are likely to feel that while they alone would have little effect on the government, their more powerful coethnics or allies are likely to be more effective.

Sometimes, of course, class and ethnicity coincide. In these cases ethnic identity provides a potential basis for unified political action; but, unless and until leadership, resources, and confidence are somehow generated, the group is likely to remain politically passive, as did American blacks, for instance, until the 1950s.

Compared to other patterns of participation, large-scale parties, unions, or movements that seek support from the poor on the basis of class-oriented appeals must make more explicit and conscious efforts to overcome the obstacles to participation. They seek wide and sustained support, and therefore they cannot be satisfied with mobilizing action around a single narrow issue (except perhaps as a starter). Nor can they rely on ethnic loyalties or on the face-to-face relationships of a small group to create trust and a capacity for collective action (although they can and sometimes do try to use local cell structures to this end). Therefore they must engage support through organization, education, shrewd selection and phasing of goals, and effective performance. And they must do all this while coping with the divergent, and sometimes conflicting, interests and prejudices of their nonpoor constituencies. It is hardly surprising that nonethnic parties, unions, and other organizations are rarely successful in mobilizing large segments of the poor.

The poor may become politically active, then, through a variety of channels—seeking different goals, utilizing different kinds of organization (or no organization at all), and having quite different implications for their own welfare and for the broader political system. It is worth exploring in greater detail the conditions that foster and shape each pattern and its variants.

Mobilized Participation

We have distinguished mobilized from autonomous political participation. (See Chapter One.) Mobilized participants, we suggested, are induced to behave in ways designed to influence the government, without being personally interested in, or even necessarily aware of, the impact of their action on the government. They are acting on instructions, and they are motivated largely or wholly by loyalty, affection, deference, or fear of a leader, or by a desire for the benefits they believe that leader may provide.

The urban and rural poor in developing countries are particularly likely to engage in mobilized rather than autonomous participation. Several different categories of leader-follower relations provide the basis for mobilization. Three of the most important of these are: ties between traditional leaders and their followers, patron-client links, and political machines. In all three categories, the links between mobilizer and mobilized tend to be face-to-face and are often based on particularized benefits for the follower (in contrast, say, to relations between a charismatic national leader and his followers).

Traditional ties are those between a following and a leader that are defined and legitimized by long-established cultural, social, or religious tradition. The most clear-cut examples are traditional African or Middle Eastern tribal chiefs and clan elders.[6] Followers, by virtue of having been born into the tribe or clan, owe allegiance to such leaders automatically, although modernized or maverick members may withhold their deference and obedience.

In the long run, traditional leaders are undoubtedly doomed, their authority eroded by colonial and national governments, economic modernization, and social change. But their influence is still substantial in parts of Africa and the Middle East, and in isolated pockets elsewhere. In some cases they have been able to transform the style of their authority and the basis of their support—becoming patrons, brokers, or the leaders of more modern communal or ethnic organizations characterized by horizontal ties among members and by autonomous participation.

While the poor and ignorant are most likely to remain faithful to traditional leaders, such leaders are more concerned with communal prerogatives and the maintenance of their own positions than with assisting the poor. Traditional leaders are more likely to respond to external threats than to initiate change independently. Moreover, since their authority rests on broad acceptance of their legitimacy, they are unlikely to resort to disruptive or even large-scale collective tactics. Negotiations, quiet consultation, coordination of elders and local influentials within their sphere of influence, petitions or delegations to higher authority, and perhaps discreet electoral campaigning are more compatible with the dignity their position requires. For a traditional leader to engage in more open competition with modern politicians, or to adopt their tactics, is not only to risk defeat in an unfamiliar game, but also to undermine his own image and authority.

Their followers owe traditional leaders respect and deference regardless of whether the leader has done them any personal favors or even knows them personally. In contrast, *patron-client links* are established individually and rest on a reciprocal but unequal exchange of benefits. The higher-status patron provides protection, economic aid, and reflected status to his clients, and intervenes on their behalf with government authorities. The clients reciprocate with loyalty and deference, labor, occasional small gifts, and political support. Because the patron-client link is more varied and adaptable to changing circumstances than traditional ties are, it is more widespread and important as a basis for mobilized participation.[7]

The prototypical patron-client relation is that between the rural landlord and his tenant or sharecropper. Particularly where one or a few landlords control all or most of the land in an area, where national government activities are confined to maintaining order and collecting taxes, and villages are physically isolated, the landlord may represent the sole source not only of land but also of work, loans, seed, livestock, and help in the event of illness, natural disasters, or trouble with government authorities. Where land is more evenly distributed, as in early twentieth century Sardinia, the cultivator may turn to the local priest, lawyer, mayor, or other local functionaries as alternatives to the handful of larger landowners.[8]

The introduction of competitive elections provides a new means for poor peasants and rural workers to repay their patrons. In rural Colombia, for example:

> Smallholders in the vicinity of large holdings, tenants, sharecroppers, day laborers and squatters alike have fashioned a *modus vivendi* with large landlords based to a greater or lesser degree on a patron-client relationship, or clientelist politics. Within the basic pattern, the local large landowner generally determined which party and candidates would be supported in his zone of influence, and in return, occasional benefits were provided for the peasantry. When

the landlord's party was in power, government jobs, road repairs, and perhaps agricultural credits might be obtained. When the landlord's party was out of power, of course, the benefits tended to flow to the loyalists of the other party.[9]

While such patterns have proved extremely durable in some cases, eventually they are eroded by modernization and evolve along any of several lines. (See Chapter Three.) It might be added, however, that the erosion of the landlord-patron's power does not necessarily free the peasant for independent political action. The peasant may now find that he depends not on one person, but on several—for example, the landlord, who still provides his land; the local party boss, who may control the flow of credit; and the storekeeper, who loaned him money when his child was ill or his daughter got married. If the interests of these three compete, the peasant may be paralyzed politically. The breakdown of conditions that permit widespread mobilized participation does not ensure that other forms of participation will automatically occur.

In urban areas, too, the poor are likely to seek patrons who can help them in times of crisis, and perhaps even provide a means of upward mobility—a loan to start a small business, references to get a job, contacts and influence to win a scholarship for a talented child. It is often suggested that such ties reflect "residual ruralism"—the replication in the city of rural patterns of dependence and deference.[10] But the insecurity of urban life for the poor, in the absence of the institutional assistance and legal protection (such as social security) available in more advanced nations, is in itself an adequate explanation for the tendency to seek better-placed friends and protectors.[11]

Urban patron-client ties rarely take the all-encompassing, long-term, and sometimes strongly affective forms characteristic of rural landlord-tenant relationships. The links in urban areas (as in modernizing rural settings) tend to be looser, more specialized, and more contingent. Possible patrons include: past and present employers; major suppliers or customers of the multitude of self-employed artisans and peddlers; shopkeepers; priests or other religious leaders; local neighborhood leaders (including but not confined to those fitting the description of the Latin American urban *cacique* or neighborhood boss); higher-status members of home-place associations or churches; and, of course, politicians and bureaucrats at all levels of the national and local hierarchy.

As the list suggests, not all urban patron-client ties have direct political implications. Some patrons are apolitical, and make no effort to influence their clients' political behavior. Others may attempt to mobilize clients only rarely and on narrow issues that affect the patron's interests directly. Still others, most obviously politician-patrons, deliberately cultivate a circle of clients as large as possible, specifically to provide political support. An aspiring politician will seek clients (and future votes) with whatever resources he can command. If he is a businessman, he may be able to offer jobs, contracts, small cash loans, or the loan of a truck or other equipment. Professionals—especially doctors and lawyers—with political aspirations can provide professional advice and services.[12] The broker's function—willingness and capacity to intercede with the authorities to help solve individual and community problems—is a common coin of politicians, whatever their other resources. And while urban politician-patrons lack the built-in territorial constituency of a large rural landlord, they will often try to establish a reputation as the friend and benefactor of whole neighborhoods or squatter settlements, providing services and trying to win government benefits, not only for individuals and families but for the community at large.

Where neighborhood-based urban politician-patrons are part of a coordinated and disciplined party, the pattern begins to approximate the classic U.S. *urban political machine*. Historically, such machines were a means for mobilizing massive participation among the urban poor. Through the ward boss, the machine offered the poor many of the same benefits a patron would provide. In exchange, the poor were expected to vote as the ward boss instructed.

The rise of the political machine in U.S. cities is usually traced to the influx of poor and ignorant immigrants, the ethnic heterogeneity of the urban populations, the broad franchise, extensive patronage, and the fragmented authority and power of urban governments, which made it difficult to meet the pressing needs of either expanding businesses or the mass of urban poor. Contemporary cities in the developing nations display many of these characteristics, and it is natural to look for at least partial replication of the machine pattern in the cities of Latin America, Africa, and Asia.

In fact, while individual politicians throughout the developing world use material inducements to win support, the fuller constellation of characteristics that enabled the political machine to mobilize the urban poor in many American cities has rarely appeared in contemporary developing nations.[13] Where machines have appeared, they have often been on a larger scale than the U.S. prototype, but less durable. Most developing nations have much more centralized party and administrative systems than the United States has, and these inhibit the development of semi-autonomous machines in individual cities. But tight discipline and authority are harder to maintain throughout a nation than in a single city. After the immediate post-independence bonanza of government jobs was allocated, and as Korean War-inflated prices for raw materials declined, many regimes found that they lacked adequate patronage and resources to run a machine. The goals of economic modernization and national unity often seem threatened by the cacophony of parochial demands evoked by machine politics. Some national machines, such as the PDCI in the Ivory Coast, have evolved in the direction of modernizing oligarchies;[14] alternatively, "amidst the ruling party's loss of support the military—which, if it could not reward, could at least punish—stepped in."[15]

Effects of mobilized participation

Although mobilized participants are not primarily concerned with influencing the government, their participation does have political implications for their own attitudes and welfare and for the broader political system.

All three types of mobilized participation have been described as bridges leading previously parochial or apolitical groups into modern municipal and national politics. The appeals and inducements (positive and negative) used by traditional leaders and patrons are familiar and comprehensible to those with little education or political experience, especially those in, or from, the countryside. And the transition from an individual patron to a personalized political party acting as a patron may be easy and natural.[16]

From the standpoint of the broader political system, followings based on traditional leadership, patron-client networks, or machines may provide a basis for the engineering of coalitions and consensus in nations where most of the population cannot yet be expected to respond to "modern" appeals to class or occupational interests, ideology, or civic duty. Such followings, in other words, permit a transitional pattern of politics and an interim basis of legitimacy. The Northern Peoples' Convention party of Northern Nigeria has been analyzed in the following terms:

> The structure of the NPC fits conveniently into this structure of traditional [clientage] relationships . . . The interlocking directorate of local administrative and party personnel inescapably bound humble persons to traditionally august figures in their capacity as party men. The dependency that derived from the vast network of clientage relationships inherent in the traditional society were transferred to the party. Loyalty to the NPC became a way of defraying traditional political obligations.[17]

To the degree that the traditional leader, patron, or machine is perceived as a broker between the individual and the government, rather than as the direct source of benefits and favors, the poor also receive a first lesson in the relevance and manipulability of government. Particularly, perhaps, in the cities, where patron-client ties tend to be specialized and contingent, loyalty takes on a conditional flavor. As long as the patron or the boss continues to be an effective source of aid, the follower or client will be faithful, but if the leader is ineffective it is not unthinkable to seek alternatives. The seeds have been planted that will grow into the idea of political support as a resource that can be used to influence the government.

What is lacking—and indeed is discouraged by these patterns of mobilization—is the notion of collective action with one's peers to influence the government. Followers of the same chief, fellow clan members, clients of the same patron, or voters in the same machine-controlled ward may or may not be friends or even know each other. Any horizontal ties they may have with one another will have little or no impact on their political behavior. How, when, and how much they participate politically is determined by each individual's ties with his leader.

Moreover, the chief, patron, or ward boss usually sees individual or collective initiative among his followers as a threat to his own preeminence. He will seek to prevent such initiative and to perpetuate his image as the indispensable intermediary.[18] From the follower's viewpoint, if the leader is perceived as the direct source of aid or the indispensable inter-mediary, there is little point in joining with peers to try to exercise influence. Moreover, mobilized participation tends to direct attention to concrete and immediate benefits—jobs, scholarships, small public works—rather than to broader legislative or executive decisions shaping policies and programs. As the mobilized follower becomes more sophisticated, he may perceive the benefits as flowing directly from the government, rather than from or through his leaders. But since the supply of benefits is limited, it is natural (and usually accurate in the short run) to see oneself as competing with one's peers for scarce rewards rather than to conceive of trying to increase the total supply through joint action.

Though the scope of benefits is limited, patron-client ties and machine politics do help to meet immediate and urgent needs of the poor. Moreover, individual patrons and the machine offer opportunities for upward mobility for the favored client and the bright and promising constituent. But the broader impact of mobilized participation is, of course, to hamper the horizontal organization and pressures needed for social reform.

Individual Contacting for Particularized Benefits

In theory, individual contacting for particularized benefits should represent the most obvious and easy form of autonomous political participation for the previously apolitical. Of all forms of political participation, individual contacting presents the most clear, direct, and (usually) immediate link between action and results. The results of other forms of participation are often uncertain, deferred in time, and diffused in incidence. No individual participant can be certain whether his action will have the desired general result, nor whether or when he will per-sonally benefit. Even though contacting may require substantial initiative and persistence, one would expect low-income people to engage in it more than in other forms of participation.

Survey data for the United States confirm this hypothesis. While contacting for particularized benefits has little overall relationship to socio-economic status (this holds also for cross-national data), citizens in the lowest third of the socio-economic scale are much more likely to engage in contacting than in other types of political activity. The bottom

Table 5.2. Low Status Americans' Participation in Particularized Contacting Compared to Other Modes of Participation

Mode of Participation	Group Average Relative to Mean for Total Population	
	Lowest sixth on SES Scale	Next-to-bottom sixth on SES Scale
Particularized Contacting	-14	+4
Overall participation scale	-46	-27
Voting	-34	-15
Campaign activity	-32	-17
Communal lobbying activity	-38	-31

SOURCE: Adapted from Sidney Verba and Norman Nie, *Participation in America* (New York: Harper & Row, 1972), Chapter 8, figures 2 and 4, pp. 132-134.

sixth of the U.S. population attempts particularized contacting less than the average citizen, but the gap between this most deprived group and the population as a whole is much narrower for contacting than for other forms of participation. The group next to the bottom in socio-economic status, interestingly enough, actually scores slightly above the overall mean for contacting, although they score substantially below average on other forms of participation.

The fact that those at the very lowest socio-economic levels do less contacting than the average citizen (although, at least in the United States, more contacting than other forms of participation) reflects at least three factors. Many of the poor simply don't know whom to contact about particular problems. Even given adequate information, the poor are often scattered in isolated rural areas where it is difficult to reach the appropriate officials. Finally, many of the very poor are undoubtedly diffident or doubtful that officials will respond favorably. These feelings are particularly strong where low-income people are also members of a subordinated ethnic group or caste; in their case, contacting requires approaching officials who are not only higher class, but also likely to be members of the dominant ethnic group. Thus, poorly educated U.S. blacks are roughly half as likely as whites of similar education to contact officials for help with individual problems. Indian Harijans with no formal education do substantially less contacting than uneducated caste Hindus.[19]

Ignorance, skepticism, and the physical or social difficulty of reaching officials all limit contacting as well as other forms of political participation among poor people in all nations. But in developing nations particularistic contacting by the poor is often restricted by another general obstacle: the comparatively narrow range of individual services and benefits available through government agencies. Wayne Cornelius found that, among low-income migrants in Mexico City, only three percent of their contacts with government officials dealt with personal or family needs. The bulk of the demands upon the government concerned neighborhood improvements.

> This low frequency of particularistic contacting . . . reflects migrants' perceptions of what types of needs are most amenable to satisfaction through governmental action. Perhaps the most important reason why individual demands for housing and employment are not frequent objects of demand-making is that the migrant usually perceives the satisfaction of such needs as an *individual* responsibility.[20]

Parallel data from Lima confirm Cornelius' findings. Even though particularized contacting theoretically has a greater appeal to the poor as a form of participation, the actual volume of contacting by the poor depends heavily on the range of government services available to them, and on their perceptions of the extent of government responsibilities.

Where services are known to exist, but people believe that officials will not respond or will demand a substantial bribe, they may seek the mediation of a more influential or affluent person. In other words, services perceived as relevant but inaccessible divert contacting into patron-client channels, thereby enlarging the potential for mobilized participation.

Small-scale Special Interest Associations

Special interest organizations among low-income people incorporate much of the logic of particularized contacting. The benefits such organizations seek are usually specific, they are perceived as squarely within the sphere of government responsibilities, and they are often of a single-shot nature. The tactics of the organizations are normally confined to various forms of petitioning. And the organizations themselves often dissolve once they achieve their goal (or if they become discouraged about achieving it). But because they use collective action, special interest organizations can pursue goals beyond the reach of individual petitioners. Organizational action also has more extensive implications than individual petitioning, both for political learning among the poor and for the broader political system.

Conditions for small-scale special interest groups

Special interest associations among the poor most commonly take the form of community development and cooperative organizations in rural areas, and neighborhood improvement associations in the cities, particularly in squatter settlements. Certain conditions must be met before such organizations can take hold.

(i) *There must be a recognized common problem that is felt to be of high priority.* Priorities are determined largely by current life situations and plans for the future. Thus, residents in a squatter community are likely to share a strong desire for piped water, electricity, and title to their lots. But if they already have water and electricity, they may care less about further community improvements—paved streets, a community center, a public telephone—than about other goals that cannot be promoted effectively through neighborhood-based collective action, such as placing a son in secondary school or achieving some job security. If many of the residents in the settlement are renters, or if many residents plan to move on to another neighborhood as soon as possible (because the settlement is inconveniently located, subject to floods or landslides, under threat of eradication, crime-ridden, etc.), then they may not be willing to invest time and energy in obtaining even basic services such as piped water. Similarly, migrants planning to return to their home villages in several years—as do many of the residents of African and South Asian towns and cities—will not give high priority to improving a residential area they regard as temporary.

(ii) *The problem must be viewed as appropriate or plausible for prompt and specific governmental action or assistance.* As noted earlier, many problems common to most low-income people are not so perceived. The problems most obviously appropriate for prompt and specific government action are those created by the government in the first place. Thus, the threat of eradication of a squatter settlement commonly triggers protest by the threatened residents. A campaign by the government of Ghana to eliminate swollen shoot disease in cocoa, its crucial export crop, by destroying diseased plants, mobilized peasant protests and obstruction on the part of farmers who had not previously been particularly active in politics. Similarly, acknowledged government responsibility for a particular task or problem causes residents to direct their appeals and efforts toward the government. In Seoul, Korea, squatters' associations are rare. But residents of low-cost "citizens' apartments," built and maintained by the municipal government to house those dislocated from eradicated squatter settlements, have formed tenants' associations that actively press the government for repairs and improvements.[21]

(iii) *There must be some assurance that the benefits will be shared equally, or at least that no one individual or clique will reap most of the rewards.* One means of providing such assurance is by the indivisible nature of the benefits sought. Alternatively, tight social cohesion may provide assurance that the benefits will be fairly shared. Such cohesion may be encouraged by a variety of factors: small or moderate group size; clear boundaries; homogeneity in ethnic background, life cycle stage, and socio-economic status; low turnover; shared experiences such as initiation of the settlement by invasion; and traditional cultural patterns of community cooperation. Finally, trusted and respected leadership can also help to provide assurance that benefits will be fairly distributed. Conversely, suspicion of the leader's motives is one of the most common obstacles to collective action in low-income communities.

(iv) *Independent participation by the poor requires leaders with some idea of how to exert influence.* In rural areas this frequently means persons with some exposure to urban experience.

(v) *Finally, collective political action must be viewed as equally or more cost-effective than alternative means.* That is, the chances of achieving the desired results through collective political action must appear as good or better, or at least the effort or risk required must appear less, than other means to the same end. The alternatives may be nonpolitical or political, individual or collective.

In Seoul, Korea, individual political channels seem to provide a partial alternative to collective action in squatter settlements. Squatter associations are rare, despite the large numbers of squatters, their comparatively high levels of education, and their ethnic homogeneity. The political climate does not encourage such associations. Equally or more important, incentives for associations are weak. The city has provided most settlements with water and electricity. Legal titles are the remaining high priority goal. At least until the early 1970s, some of the more affluent squatters were apparently able to acquire title individually, by negotiating with (and undoubtedly paying) the appropriate authorities. This was a more direct and probably a less risky means of obtaining title than collective political efforts.[22]

In Chile and in Peru, collective self-help, rather than individual contacts and bribes, seems to have been the major alternative to collective lobbying for neighborhood improvements. In Lima before 1970, the government was not very responsive to pressures from squatter groups, although new settlements were tacitly permitted (and sometimes even encouraged) and certain agencies did provide sporadic and unpredictable assistance. Squatters relied substantially on communal self-help, raising funds and contributing labor to build sidewalks, lay water pipes, and the like. Legal titles, however, could not be attained through self-help, and in 1968 a sizeable demonstration was organized to demand titles. In Chile until 1973, government agencies and politicians were much more responsive to pressures from the urban poor than they were in Peru, and neighborhood associations relied less on self-help and more on lobbying and petitioning for needed improvements.

In principle, squatters seeking legal title and better housing conditions could consider, as alternatives to collective political action, not only individual contacts and collective self-help but also moving, or exit. But since legal housing within the financial reach of the urban poor is very scarce in most developing nations, this option is usually blocked.

To summarize: The poor take political action through small-scale special interest groups only where such action seems to be a reasonable approach to a recognized, common, and high-priority problem; where community cohesiveness and the nature of the goal inspire confidence that all will benefit; and where alternative individual or collective approaches do not appear more promising. These conditions can normally be met only in small local areas. Organization over large areas requires leadership and resources not available to the poor without external aid. Moreover, suspicions and internal divisions multiply as participation expands to include people who are strangers to each other. In small neighborhoods and communities, suspicions are to some extent dispelled by mutual surveillance.

Goals of special interest groups among the poor

Rural and urban areas differ with respect to the kinds of issues around which organizations may coalesce. Rural participation may focus on community improvements or on the common concerns of those who engage in specific economic activities (hand weavers, small coffee growers) or share an economic status (tenant farmers). Urban efforts more frequently focus on physical improvements and services for the neighborhood, since the wider range and greater instability of occupations complicates cooperation organized around economic interests.

Rural and urban areas are similar, however, in the nature of the goals sought by small-scale special interest organizations of the poor. Such organizations almost always seek concrete, often single-shot benefits—physical improvements like a well, road, or water-main; specific concessions such as legal recognition and land titles for a squatter area; more rarely, credit or a loan to start a cooperative or to finance a communal facility. As noted earlier, small-scale collective participation may also be spurred by a threat to common interests from the government itself, from other private groups, or from natural forces such as flood or erosion. In all of these cases, petitioning by low-income groups is the collective analog of individual contacting; both are ways of seeking specific concrete benefits or emergency assistance.

Attempts to exert broader political influence are extremely rare. Seldom does a small group of poor people seek to alter government policies or to affect the design or scale of governmental programs. For example, squatters' associations may press for recognition for their neighborhoods, but they almost never lobby, singly or in cooperation with other associations, for or against the provisions of a bill establishing criteria for legalizing settlements. Community groups may petition authorities to gravel an access road or arrange more frequent bus service for their area, but would not attempt to influence the size of appropriations or the criteria guiding road construction or bus service in general.

Tactics of special interest groups among the poor

The logic of the situation limits the tactics that small groups are likely to employ. Most frequent is the petitioning of legislators and agencies at the local, state or provincial, and national level. In Chile under Frei and Allende, for example, the halls and anterooms of key officials in agencies responsible for housing, electricity, roads and sewers, education, health, and related services were crowded every afternoon, during hours open to the public, with delegations from various *poblaciones.*

Groups may also enlist the local press and radio to help their cause. The newspapers in many cities in developing nations run columns on "the neighborhoods" or "local news," which detail the problems of particular communities or the self-help efforts and appeals for help of specific groups. For example, in 1965 a small barrio in Ciudad Guayana, Venezuela, became aware that a large sewer was under construction nearby. The sewer would empty into the river close to the spot used by the barrio residents, as well as others, for bathing and laundry. The first appeal of the concerned residents was through the newspapers and radio. The barrio had no idea who was responsible for the planning and construction of the sewer, but in this first stage aimed their protest at "the competent authorities." Their next step was a determined effort to locate and contact, or petition, the appropriate authorities.[23]

Tactics other than petitioning and publicity are rarer. Where political competition makes even small numbers of votes important, associations or organizations use the promise of political support to try to win the intervention of politicians. Such action has been taken by squatter associations in Chile, Brazil (prior to 1964), and Venezuela, among other places.[24] In desperate circumstances, groups may resort to demonstrations or to illegal or violent actions designed to dramatize their plight and exert pressure on authorities to act. One group of squatters in Santiago, displaced from their original location, camped in the center of a major highway, disrupting traffic for weeks, insisting that they be provided with suitable land on which to settle. A few residents of the Venezuelan barrio just described, frustrated by their inability to persuade authorities to halt construction of the sewer fouling their stretch of river bank (or indeed even to pay any attention to their problem), poured sand into the carburetors of the construction machinery one night while the watchman slept. Such incidents, however, are unusual, as one would expect in view of the small size of the groups, their lack of political influence, and their basic goals—persuading the authorities to provide a specific facility or service as a matter of good will, special favor, or at least nonroutine procedure.

Not only are the goals of small interest groups narrow and their tactics moderate, but their efforts are normally short-lived or sporadic. Many studies of community development, neighborhood organizations, and other forms of political action among the urban poor in the United States, have analyzed the dynamics of starting and sustaining such efforts.[25] Given the initial cynicism and apathy of groups of poor people, the internal divisions, and the distrust of their own leaders, it is difficult to engage them in collective action. Once engaged, they are easily discouraged. Paradoxically, even success threatens the life of the organization. Often, authorities agree to take an action but fail to follow through, or do so only partially or after long delay. The initial concession deflates group pressure and momentum, while the failure to implement confirms earlier cynicism. Concessions from the authorities sometimes entail the community's taking partial responsibility for implementation. This is especially true of on-going services such as cooperatives or schools. The skills required to manage a continuing operation are not the same as those required to mount a lobbying campaign. Maintaining and operating a facility or service often overstrains limited leadership capacity. Finally, and most frequently, if the goal sought is specific and single-shot, victory destroys the *raison d'être* of the organization. Unless the leaders can quickly transfer the enthusiasm and momentum to new goals, the organization disintegrates. As a result, urban neighborhood associations have a distinct tendency to die as a neighborhood becomes established and basic facilities are provided.[26]

Federations of interest groups

In theory, federations of local independent associations at the municipal, provincial, or national level should be able to embrace more members and territory, address a wider range of issues, maintain greater continuity, and exercise greater autonomy than individual associations can. But the impediments to the organization of federations are much the same as those that limit scale and scope at the local level—lack of resources and leadership, distrust and rivalry among localities, and the belief that collective action at the level of a federation is unlikely to produce more or quicker results than independent action by localities.

In the urban sector, settlements vary widely in their social and economic composition, and in the extent to which they have become established as part of the larger metropolitan community. The residents of higher-level and better established settlements or sections of settlements often look down upon the poorer and more marginal groups. The very cohesion that sustains effective organization at the community level is often translated into rivalry among neighborhoods. A small *poblacion* in Santiago was determined to have a clinic on its own territory, even though a new clinic had recently opened in a neighboring settlement within easy walking distance. Moreover, settlements tend to assume that resources are scarce and static, so that one settlement gains only at the expense of others. This is a natural outlook in systems where benefits flow largely as the result of special ties, petitioning, or bargaining for political support.

Under some conditions, joint action among urban low-income residents does occur. In the summer of 1968, thousands of barriada residents in Lima organized and carefully rehearsed a march on the Presidential Palace to demand that they be granted title to their land. The titles were granted. A strong and widely known leader had organized the demonstration, and the issue of titles was not merely relevant but central for virtually all the settlers. There was already a legal basis for providing title, but execution had been stalled for years. The problem looked like one that could be solved (or at any rate eased) by a stroke of the pen. Conditions, in short, were ideal. However, later efforts by the same leader to organize further demonstrations around other issues failed. The show of unity was a single-shot effort, more fragile than most neighborhood associations.

Stronger independent federations are likely to be repressed. In Rio de Janeiro, the Federation of Associations of Favela Residents of the State of Guanabara (FAFEG) was formed in 1964; by 1968 it represented at least 100 favelas in the city. FAFEG directed attention not only to state-wide issues but also to national issues affecting favela residents, and it focused on policies rather than immediate outputs. In 1968, a powerful agency of the Federal Government adopted an active policy of favela clearance and relocation. FAFEG reacted sharply against the new policy in its state-wide congress of that year, and also moved to block action against the first of the favelas threatened with removal. The officers of FAFEG were promptly arrested and held incommunicado for several days. They were released only after pressure from the more liberal wing of the Catholic church in Rio. After the mass arrest, there were no further efforts to halt the eradication of favelas in the south zone of the city.[27]

Local associations, outside aid, and autonomy

Local organizations of the poor are a favorite focus for assistance from charitable or religious groups—middle-class and elite—from government agencies interested in promoting the welfare of low-income groups, and from foreign benefactors. There are three reasons for this interest. First, from the point of view of those concerned with increasing welfare, such assistance can potentially improve living conditions and increase the incomes of some of the most deprived groups in the society. Funds from private and foreign benefactors can go more or less directly to those who need help, without passing through (and being diverted by) echelons of bureaucrats. Second, from the standpoint of promoting development, the self-help component of small-scale local action mobilizes labor, ideas, local managerial capacity, and savings not available for other forms of investment; in the economist's terms, the opportunity costs are very low. Third, small organizations of the poor do not threaten the position of those already in power (other than local patrons or bosses) or create pressure for substantial reorientation of government priorities and programs. They do not seriously challenge the status quo.

Most private, and much public, support for independent organizations among the poor is channeled through community development programs. Traditionally, such programs shun not only partisan activity but all political activity. They rely as fully as possible on self-help with limited assistance, normally channeled through the supporting agency itself or provided by other public or private agencies at the request of the community development agency acting as coordinator. Governmental programs like Promoción Popular, under the Frei administration in Chile, and the Community Action Program of the Office of Economic

Opportunity in the United States, departed from traditional community development philosophy. They advocated organization among low-income groups not only to facilitate self-help, but also to exercise greater influence on government decision-making. That is, they encouraged collective political participation among previously unorganized and voiceless social groups. Promocion Popular originated as an arm of the Christian Democratic Party, and in its early stages was used rather blatantly to gain support for the Frei regime in poor urban neighborhoods. This partisan use of the program caused opposition members of the Congress to refuse to pass legislation designed to convert Promocion Popular into an official government program. In addition to the partisan motives for the program, however, Christian Democratic ideology strongly emphasized the importance of widespread popular participation as a general principle. Moreover, neighborhood councils had existed in Chile long before Promocion Popular, and support for a greater neighborhood voice in local government affairs was strong among all parties. Legislation to regularize and strengthen the councils' position in both poor and non-poor neighborhoods was passed with support from all parties; at the same time, Promocion Popular was denied legislative sanction.

In many countries, private institutions concerned with the welfare of the poor, particularly church groups in some Latin American nations, increasingly regard political action by the poor as an appropriate and perhaps essential supplement to more traditional reliance on charity and self-help efforts. In this sense they have moved beyond traditional community development theory. However, such governmental or private efforts usually retain the more traditional approach of avoiding partisan entanglement, as least in principle.

Local associations, government regulation, and autonomy

A variety of governmental measures may serve to stimulate local associations. The most direct and simple means is to grant legal recognition. In Rio, for example, most of the favela associations date from the early 1960s, when the Directorate of Social Services for the state of Guanabara undertook a program to create associations and grant full citizenship to all residents of Rio. Legal information and the services of lawyers were provided to assist in drawing up association constitutions.[28]

Chile long had a procedure through which neighborhood councils could gain legal recognition, but the complex and lengthy arrangements discouraged all but a handful from gaining recognition. The procedure was substantially simplified by legislation passed in mid-1968.

Although legal recognition offers advantages (for example, in Chile, being able to borrow money from the banks), it usually also entails meeting certain criteria designed to ensure that the associations are representative and honestly administered. The Chilean law included minutely detailed requirements regarding nomination and election of council members, specifying, for example, the minimum number of posters to be posted announcing an election and the minimum number of days they were to be displayed in advance of the election. In Rio de Janeiro in the late 1960s, the atmosphere toward neighborhood associations in low-income areas was as hostile as Chile's was supportive. Regulations regarding recognition were clearly designed for control; favela associations were recognized only if they represented more than half of their residents, and each association had to file a list of all residents in the favela, as well as a quarterly financial report. Similarly detailed regulations and close supervision are typical of officially-sponsored rural cooperative programs.[29] Whether intended to control or assist, detailed requirements stifle local initiative.

Beyond the problem of overregulation, whether in the name of assistance or control, is the problem of coöptation. National and municipal governments, parties, and other institutions face tremendous problems in opening and maintaining lines of communication and information with low-income citizens in both rural and urban settings. Middle- and upper-income strata are more highly organized and conduct more of their business in recorded or otherwise accessible forms; more importantly, informal sources of information and two-way communication are readily available. In low-income areas, however, it is often hard to know what is going on, just as it is often extremely difficult for low-income people, individually or collectively, to get information from the authorities or to locate those responsible for particular programs.

Both problems are neatly illustrated in the account of "the great sewer controversy" mentioned earlier. The residents of the barrio had great difficulty discovering what agency and officials were responsible for construction of the sewer; talks with the men at the construction site, a visit to the office of the state governor, and repeated inquiries in the offices of various agencies were necessary before the proper official was finally located. Moreover, once he was contacted, his reaction was high-handed and unresponsive. Shortly thereafter, however, he did attempt to meet with the barrio people to discuss the problem. He contacted the ostensible head of the barrio community council and asked that a meeting be called. Unfortunately,

> the council was in this period more or less moribund, and its head, the agent of the dominant political party, was, despite his clearly party-politician role, a person of very minimal political skills who had been living outside of the barrio for a year. He was so out of touch with recent events . . . that he failed to gather together more than a handful of people for the meeting.[30]

The official, of course, had no way of knowing that he had entirely failed to get in touch with the concerned community.

Some sort of officially sanctioned and regulated local organization that represents its constituents is thus important as a means for municipal and higher government authorities to communicate with the people and execute policies, regardless of whether those policies are designed primarily to aid or to control. In Lima in 1961, legislation was passed to legalize existing settlements and to forbid the creation of further settlements. The procedures for legalization depended heavily on formation of barriada councils. In Rio, in the late 1960s, favela associations not only had to submit a file of residents in the settlement, but were also responsible, in theory, for making cadastral surveys, controlling repairs on houses, and preventing new building! The temptation to coöpt the local associations and use them for governmental purposes can enter into even the most supportive program. In Chile, for example, the 1968 legislation included an option designed to help associations raise revenue by collecting rents or fees owed by residents to government agencies (for example, house rents owed to the Housing Corporation). The associations would retain a 7% commission. One cannot help but wonder what effect this function would have had on the councils' apparent, if not real, autonomy in the eyes of their constituents.

If coöptation is an ever-present danger, powerful political antagonism is a threat that grows in direct proportion to the success and true autonomy of a local association. Experience with the O.E.O. Community Action Program in the United States makes plain that local authorities will not hesitate to exercise a variety of repressive measures aimed directly at the offending association, and to appeal to higher levels of government to bring the troublemakers into line. Few local associations have the resources to stand against such opposition.

Effects of small-scale special interest organizations

The political implications of small special interest groups among the poor are broader than those of individual contacting, but analogous in several respects. Both individual contacting and participation through small interest groups produce some benefits for the poor. Indeed, the frequency and volume of both types of participation probably reflect the probability of success. But unless the aggregate volume of individual or small-group demands by the poor is very high, such participation is not likely to significantly affect the broader political system, either in terms of the allocation of public resources and priorities, or in terms of the distribution of power. A system where most low-income participation is confined to contacting or small interest groups operates to maintain the status quo. Pressures that might otherwise take a collective form, and be directed to earlier stages of policy formation or to the composition of the government itself, are diverted into discrete, separable and small demands, which can be met, in full or in part, or rejected one by one.

Small interest groups can, however, have a substantial impact on the political attitudes and perceptions of their members. Cornelius studied how the experience of attempting to influence the government affected the political attitudes of migrants in six neighborhoods in Mexico City. He examined these efforts for all of his respondents as a group, and also for separate groups from each neighborhood. Controlling for the effects of age, socio-economic status, and length of urban experience, he found for the respondents as a whole that contacts with the government and receipt of personal services related positively and moderately strongly to feelings of personal political efficacy, pride in and identification with national political institutions, general support for the political system, and perception of the government as responsive to citizen pressure. However, as one would expect, negative contact with the government—that is, unsuccessful attempts to gain collective or individual benefits—related negatively to these political attitudes.[31]

Looking at residents of the six neighborhoods as separate groups,

Cornelius also found considerable variation in the proportions reporting various types of political activity and scoring high on various indicators of political involvement. These contrasts persisted even after controlling for variation among the neighborhoods with respect to average age, educational level, length of urban experience, and general interest in politics. The differences were best explained by contrasts in each neighborhood's leadership, political history, and relations with the authorities. In other words, the neighborhood acts as an agent for political instruction. The lessons taught by well organized and effective neighborhoods confronting reasonably responsive authorities differ from those taught by poorly organized neighborhoods confronting unresponsive authorities.[32] Similarly, studies of four neighborhoods in Santiago, Chile, and Lima, Peru, traced substantial differences in political attitudes to sharply varying political experiences in each neighborhood.[33] Related findings have been reported for a comparative study of Panama City, Guayaquil, and Lima, and for an extensive analysis of squatter settlements in Lima.[34] Survey data from three squatter settlements in Istanbul also suggest parallel findings, although the analysis itself does not focus on variation in attitudes among the three neighborhoods.[35]

Successful experience in participating through small interest groups can heighten political efficacy. But the long-term effects on attitudes and behavior remain to be explored. We have seen that the forms, goals, and duration of such groups tend to be quite limited. To what extent can attitudes shaped by successful experience with a neighborhood association, rural cooperative, or other small local organization be transferred to participation organized on different bases, using different techniques, and seeking different goals? To the best of our knowledge, no studies have yet addressed this question.

Cross-class Participation

To make a substantial impact on the political system usually requires larger-scale and more sustained participation than contacting or special interest groups among the poor can generate. For our purposes it is convenient to divide larger-scale participation by the poor into two broad categories: cross-class and poor-oriented. Both categories usually involve middle-class or elite leadership, and participation by nonpoor in collaboration with segments of the poor. The differences revolve around the nature of the goals sought. Cross-class patterns are discussed in this section; poor-oriented patterns in the next.

The most obvious and clear-cut cases of cross-class participation among the poor occur in ethnically divided nations. Where cleavages of tribe, region, religion, or language cut across class lines, political organization and issues are often dominated by such cleavages. Communal loyalties and ethnic parties are likely to provide the main channel through which poorly educated and low-income groups are brought into politics. Ethnic emotions can generate extremely high participation rates at all socio-economic levels. In Guyana, for example, tensions between East Indians and Negroes peaked in the early 1960's; the turnout for the general elections of 1961 was 89.4 per cent; in 1964 the turnout reached 96.9 per cent of the electorate.[36] Political participation based on ethnic identity is often very emotional and is probably more violence-prone than other patterns of participation.

Cross-class participation by the poor reflects a blend of mobilization, material self-interest, and communal loyalties. Political leadership, in divided no less than in homogeneous societies, is almost wholly in the hands of the middle and upper classes. Within each ethnic community, poorer members are likely to depend economically, as well as politically, on their more fortunate coethnics. In rural areas, land, employment, and credit all are linked to ethnic ties; in urban areas, jobs and often housing may be channeled virtually entirely through ethnic mechanisms. Particular government agencies or offices, specific private firms, and whole fields of economic activity are the preserves of particular ethnic groups. Even if a quota system evolves in some fields or agencies, well-positioned members of each ethnic group control the allocation of their quota to less influential coethnics.

Thus, in societies where ethnic divisions cut across class lines, the low-income agricultural worker, subsistence farmer, or urban worker may be encouraged to vote or demonstrate by his coethnic landlord, employer, village elder, or ward boss, and may act largely or partly from respect or fear. But the same person is also likely to feel a real sense of communal loyalty, and a reluctance or anger at the prospect of "the others" taking power. Moreover, while he may resent more fortunate coethnics and believe they are haughty and unresponsive to his needs, he probably sees his own immediate material welfare and long-run prospects associated with communal political power. If his coethnic relatives and acquaintances lose their civil service positions, he and his sons or nephews lose the possibility of jobs as clerks or janitors. More broadly, policies that increase the opportunities for his community are desirable even if the immediate impact on his own life is minimal or, perhaps, negative. The Malay rice cultivator is not likely to gain personally from a language policy that permits the use of Malay for university entrance examinations. But his bright nephew may benefit; in any case, the policy increases opportunity for Malays. Moreover, the issue has symbolic importance. The Indian laborer on a sugar estate in Guyana does not benefit from rice marketing-board policies that raise the price of rice. Indeed, he may have to pay more for his staple food. But most rice farmers are Indian. Perhaps the sugar worker dreams of acquiring a few acres and becoming a rice farmer himself some day.[37]

In short, ethnic loyalty is a powerful factor activating low-income members of ethnic communities, even though their middle-class or elite leaders are not likely to focus on the special problems and needs of the urban or rural poor. As a corollary, leftist parties in general do extremely poorly among low-income groups in areas where ethnic ties are politically salient and cut across class lines.[38]

Even in ethnically homogeneous societies, certain cross-class issues may generate participation among the poor. In the past, anti-colonial movements received support from all strata of society, although low-income and poorly-educated groups were in most cases underrepresented. After independence, overall levels of participation often dropped sharply. In independent nations, an external threat can prompt the poor, as well as the more affluent, to demonstrations of patriotic zeal, designed usually to encourage and support the government, or sometimes to rouse it to a more energetic defense of national interests.

Narrower issues can also crystallize cross-class collaboration and engage elements of the poor. Inflation in general, and particularly increases in the prices of staple foods and bus fares, are likely to arouse the ire of lower, lower-middle, and middle-class groups alike. Moreover, the same corrective actions can be sought by different classes. Underemployment and unemployment, in contrast, seldom provide a focus for cross-class cooperation, even though both the lower and lower-middle classes are affected. Unlike inflation, unemployment takes different forms in different socio-economic strata. The truly poor, especially those with dependents, cannot afford to remain unemployed; instead, they accept insecure and badly paid jobs. Open employment is disproportionately concentrated among young men with middle or even higher levels of education. In Latin America and parts of Asia, this may mean high-school graduates; in Lagos or Nairobi it may mean those who have completed elementary school, the so-called "seventh standard boys."[39] The point is not merely that some groups are underemployed or badly employed, and others openly unemployed, but that they differ in the kinds of jobs they will accept, and hence in the types of governmental action they view as necessary. Therefore, a coalition built on issues of employment is more difficult to create than one focused on staple prices.

Political participation triggered by specific issues that cut across class lines tends to take the form of demonstrations. The demonstrations may be in support of the government, as is usually the case in nationalist crises, or in protest against rising prices or other issues. The latter may become violent. Such issues, of course, are also grist for campaign mills. Populist political leaders, in particular, are likely to campaign in low-income areas on issues of rising prices and the need for public works to generate employment, while appealing to groups a few steps higher up the socio-economic ladder with the same attacks on inflation, somewhat different proposals regarding employment, and additional issues such as inequitable patterns of taxation.

Effects of cross-class participation

Cross-class participation, by definition, is not addressed to needs specific to the poor. Nonetheless, the organizers of parties or movements based on cross-class appeals such as anti-colonialism or ethnicity often appeal to low-income groups not only on the basis of shared patriotism or ethnic loyalty but also on the grounds that their opponents—the colonial or former colonial power, or rival ethnic groups—are denying their group its rightful economic and social opportunities. However, the concrete policies and programs demanded by cross-class parties or movements usually benefit the middle class much more than the poor.

Cross-class participation may affect the political attitudes of poor participants more than their welfare. Ethnic parties in ethnically divided societies are probably the most potent form of organization for politicizing the poor and the poorly educated. This is true not only in today's developing nations but also in the United States, in the present as well as the past. Even cross-class participation that is not based on ethnic loyalties may encourage greater interest in politics and a belief in the potential influence of unified and determined participation. Attitudes encouraged by nonethnic cross-class participation—as compared to the political awareness and efficacy generated by ethnic ties—may be more readily transferred to other patterns, such as small-scale interest groups or parties oriented to the lower classes.

Large-scale Organizations Oriented to the Lower Classes

The channels of participation that are most likely to encourage some revision of development priorities in favor of the less privileged are, obviously enough, parties and other organizations that focus on the problems of low-income people as a social class. Indeed, the notion of "participation by the poor" is often used to imply this kind of focus. In its extreme versions, this participation is the social revolutionary's dream and the conservative's nightmare. In its various Marxist variations, such participation rests, in principle, on growing class consciousness. This consciousness, however, is not automatic: it calls for pervasive indoctrination, and is often a result, rather than a cause, of radical regimes' taking power. More moderate and less class-conscious versions of class-based participation are organized by peasant unions, occasional farmer-worker parties, and, to a certain extent, by labor unions. Class-based participation is most likely to emerge in societies approximating the populist model of development.

Obstacles to large-scale political organization oriented to the poor

Since the rural and urban poor constitute the great majority of the population in most developing nations, they would appear to be an obvious political resource. Moreover, development is associated with a long-run trend toward class-based politics. (See Chapter 3.) Yet, with the exception of the less developed communist nations, there have been remarkably few serious and sustained efforts to organize and capitalize on the potential support of the poor, except on the basis of cross-class appeals such as nationalism or ethnicity. And where attempts have been made to organize the poor, they have usually been short-lived and ineffective. In other words, while the middle classes and organized labor usually enter politics as classes at fairly early stages, the poor are seldom brought into the political arena as a class until quite late, if at all.

Why are effective class-based appeals to the masses so rare? The problems lie both in motivation and in organization.

The poor are difficult for outsiders to organize. All the impediments to independent organization among the poor—skepticism about the pertinence of political action, internal divisions, unstable jobs and residences in urban areas, limited time and energy and funds—also hamper parties and unions. Often, moreover, middle-class and elite biases and ignorance compound the problems. Party workers may believe that slums and squatter settlements are hotbeds of social disorganization, vice, and crime, and they may be reluctant to work there. Rural organizers must usually be recruited from rural or small town residents (some of whom may have had some urban experience), since urbanites are likely to regard rural assignments as tantamount to exile. Once in contact with the poor, the organizers' attitudes of distaste, fear, or paternalism are difficult to overcome and to conceal. However, the most important problems facing an aspiring outside organizer of the poor have to do with resources and staying power rather than mannerisms. Before the poor will respond, they must be convinced that the outsider has the contacts and the resources to accomplish something useful to them, and that he will stay long enough to follow through and protect them from reprisals.[40]

Conflicting priorities are a second problem. Few sizeable political organizations or movements are primarily concerned with low-income people. Some (though not all) socialist and communist parties are concerned; most, however, divide their appeal between low-income groups and the more secure and comfortable working-class strata of organized industrial labor. Some non-Marxist parties, usually those based largely on middle-class support, may be influenced by ideology or competition, or both, to broaden their appeal to encompass low-income workers or peasants. Such parties have multiple interests and objectives that are often inconsistent. Peasant syndicates are often branches of parties that embrace a range of classes. Moreover, even within their own ranks some syndicates attempt to ally small- and medium-sized independent farmers, subsistence farmers, and agricultural workers in a (usually uneasy) coalition. In short, improving the situation of the poor is rarely the sole or even the major goal of parties and unions, even those that make a serious attempt to organize support among the poor.

In pursuing new sources of support, established parties and other organizations must take care not to alienate old supporters. Urban party organizations in the United States sought to mobilize black in-migrants during the 1940s and 1950s, but they were initially reluctant to elevate black politicians to positions of responsibility within the city hierarchy. The Democratic party today is more broadly torn between the desire to appeal to underprivileged groups and the imperative need to hold lower-middle-class and established working-class support. Church groups, in the United States and elsewhere, whose concern for the poor and for minorities has led them to advocate and encourage political participation by the poor, have risked antagonizing their lower-middle-class members.

In modernizing nations, this problem applies particularly clearly to the role of labor unions vis-a-vis the urban poor. In much of Latin America, Africa, and Asia, the urban population is growing at rates of five to eight percent a year, or even more rapidly, while employment in modern manufacturing enterprises expands at roughly three to four percent annually, at best. Unions are strongest and best organized, in general, in those segments of manufacturing and services that are characterized by large, modern, and often foreign-owned units. Workers in such enterprises are more skilled, more secure, earn more in wages and fringe benefits, and are better protected through existing labor legislation than the much larger fraction of the urban working force that is employed in small-scale manufacturing, in domestic or other personal services, construction work, day labor, or peddling, not to mention the large numbers of wholly unemployed. The unions, in other words, represent a labor elite. While this has always been the case to some degree, in industrialized as well as modernizing nations, the size of the labor elite relative to the total urban working force is smaller, and the gap in living standards between it and the lower stratum is wider in many developing nations than it has ever been in the industrialized nations. The interests of this labor elite clearly conflict with the interests of the less privileged majority on issues of wages and employment, though not necessarily on other issues, such as prices of staple consumer goods. Unions and union leaders concentrate on preserving their favored position; they tend to be indifferent or even somewhat hostile to the interests of the urban poor.

Conditions for lower-class oriented appeals

In view of the difficulties of organizing either rural or urban poor on any substantial scale, and the risks of alienating established supporters in the process, powerful motivations are required to push parties, governments, or unions into a serious bid for sustained low-income support. The most common motivations are strong political competition or intense ideological commitment by party leaders. In the absence of one or the other, there may be sporadic and superficial bids for support—campaign speeches in low-income areas, perhaps a barbecue or the distribution of clothing or toys in an urban slum—but no sustained organizational effort or commitment in terms of policies and programs.

The two nations in Latin America where parties have most energetically and systematically pursued the support of urban and rural poor (as distinct from organized industrial labor) are Venezuela and Chile. In Venezuela, from the mid-1930s, the middle-class leadership of Acción Democrática worked hard to build mass support in urban as well as rural areas. Their period of control from 1945 to 1948 enabled them to consolidate rural support by providing rural benefits. During the period of Pérez Jiménez's authoritarian rule, they were better able to maintain their rural than their urban cadres. After the fall of Pérez Jiménez, both opposition parties and AD competed vigorously for control of municipal councils and the votes of the low-income barrios. Moreover, the Christian Democrats, impressed by the success of AD in the rural areas, began to press for rural support in the one region where they already had some strength; not only were they successful in this region, but they later moved to challenge the AD monopoly in other rural areas.

In Chile, strong competition, coupled with ideology, led Marxist parties in the late 1950s and early 1960s to systematically develop ties with low-income urban neighborhoods, and to seek similar influence among agricultural workers as well as among the organized mining and industrial unions that long had been their stronghold. The Christian Democrats followed suit in the 1960s, and more conservative parties also were pressed into bidding for *poblacion* votes.

In northern Italy a partly parallel pattern evolved. The Italian Communist party was the first to perceive and respond to massive rural-to-urban and south-to-north migration. In the 1950s and earlier, it had supported legislation, dating from the Mussolini era, that restricted movement from the countryside into the cities. As northern Italy's economic boom reduced the threat that in-migration posed to the wages of established workers, who constituted a major part of the Communist party's support, and as the dimensions of the migration began to become apparent, the party moved to revise its position. Conferences on migration were held as early as 1957; in 1962 the party organized "a highly effective campaign to aid the incoming migrants and to become the political party of the migrants à la Tammany Hall. The Communists became the major political force in the immigrant neighborhoods, with a practical monopoly of propaganda, organization, and initiative."[41] Catholic organizations followed suit shortly after the Communist party initiative, recognizing both the scope of the new social problem and the political threat.

The strategy of ANAPO in Colombia was similarly a product of intense competition and perceived opportunity, although the element of ideological commitment was, at best, much weaker. ANAPO sought to break into a political arena dominated by two traditional parties operating within a constitutional arrangement that shielded them from any, save internal or splinter, opposition. (See Chapter 3.) The neglected poor, especially in the cities, appeared the most likely to support Rojas Pinilla's challenge to the establishment. And in 1970 energetic organization and campaigning in low-income urban districts did indeed bring ANAPO within a hair's breadth of capturing the presidency.[42]

If ANAPO's appeals to the poor reflected competition more than ideology, the role of the liberal Church in many Latin American nations reflects commitment more than competition. (Concern over communist inroads is, however, also a factor prompting Church receptivity to social change.) While the Church has long been a conservative bastion, younger and more liberal and even radical elements have steadily gained in power. They received a strong assist from the Vatican's new commitment to social (though not doctrinal) change embodied in the encyclicals of Pope John XXIII and the 1967 *Populorum Progressio* of Pope Paul VI. In the Dominican Republic, for example, the Church was instrumental in organizing, supporting and protecting a Federation of Peasant Leagues, starting almost immediately after the assassination of the dictator Rafael Trujillo in 1961. In the province of Veraguas in Panama, Bishop McGrath and the Church played a key role in nurturing a promising co-operative movement. In Northeast Brazil, Archbishop Dom Helder Pessao Camara and others within the Church organized peasant leagues to compete with the Ligas Campesinas established by Socialist state deputy Francisco Juliao. The military regime that took power in 1964 dissolved the Ligas and exiled Juliao, but Dom Helder continued to organize rural unions and train their leaders in means of seeking non-violent basic reform.[43]

Both for political parties and for institutions such as the Church, the desire to organize the rural or the urban poor must be matched with resources to win and hold their support. The wealth and influence of the Church clearly place it in an excellent position to support and protect fledgling (and not so fledgling) organizations, in those nations where the Church hierarchy is disposed to support social change. Lacking comparable independent (and, to some extent, external) wealth and prestige, political parties usually must gain control over the resources of government if they are to sustain and expand support among the poor. In Venezuela, for example, the provisional government that replaced Pérez Jiménez in 1958 launched a massive Plan de Emergencia to create jobs and channel resources to low-income urbanites, partly in order to meet the high expectations for improvement after the dictator's fall. But opposition parties, strong in low-income neighborhoods, used the resources to consolidate their claim to leadership in the barrios. When the elected government controlled by Acción Democrática took office in 1959, it soon terminated the Plan de Emergencia, and opposition-controlled councils in urban barrios were thereafter starved for resources.

However, national control alone was not enough; in Caracas and other cities where the opposition controlled the municipal governments, efforts to substitute AD for opposition leadership at the neighborhood level ran into serious difficulties.[44] In short, parties in power are in the best position to make a credible bid for support among the poor; their effectiveness is greater if they control both national and local levels of government. With the exception of revolutionary regimes, however, parties in power are rarely motivated to appeal to the poor, unless they feel insecure and view a broadened power base as the best strategy for consolidating their position. (See Chapter 2.)

Effects of lower-class oriented participation

When large-scale political organizations oriented to lower-class needs seek and gain power, they can bring about radical changes in favor of their constituents. Short of revolution, appeals to lower-class support, in combination with other strata, can sometimes be a winning political strategy, and can also exert some influence on governmental actions. Acción Democrática rose to power in Venezuela largely through successful organization of the peasantry. The Christian Democratic victory in Chile in 1964 owed much to support from low-income urban settlements, as did Allende's narrow plurality in 1970, though both candidates drew the majority of their support from other socio-economic groups. Moreover, class-oriented participation generates pressure on the organizers to alter their own priorities and programs in ways responsive to the needs of their low-income supporters. This is true whether or not the organizers are ideologically inclined in that direction. Because large-scale class-based organization is usually attempted under conditions of intense political competition, organizers seldom can afford to jettison low-income support even after they have won power. Even where the party or movement does not gain power, a strong showing may produce concessions from victorious opponents. Thus, ANAPO's near-win in Colombia in 1970 generated a great deal of concern in traditional party circles and prompted some action to ease urban poverty. Large-scale participation generated by lower-class-oriented appeals is likely to modify the style and substance of national politics, substantially if the party or movement takes power, more subtly and gradually if it merely makes a good showing.

Participation by the poor in response to class-oriented appeals is also likely to affect the attitudes and political perceptions of the participants. Standard theory argues that people must view politics as relevant and their own participation as potentially effective, as a prerequisite to political participation. (See Chapter 4.) However, survey research among Venezuelan peasants suggests that low-income people who lack these attitudes may nonetheless join organizations focused on their problems, and that active membership in vigorous and effective organizations of this kind may create feelings of relevance and efficacy with respect to politics. The surveys found that many peasants joined peasant syndicates in the vague expectation that the syndicate might help to improve their conditions, but without any clear sense of their capacity to influence government decisions. But peasants who had belonged to a peasant union for some time were much more likely than those who had never been members to believe that they could influence the government. More specifically, those who had belonged to active and effective unions, and who took an active part themselves in union affairs, were likely to feel able to influence the political system: participation created a sense of efficacy rather than the other way around.[45]

It is hardly surprising that participation by the poor, through sizeable and durable organizations that are focused partly or largely on their problems, is the most effective channel for altering the attitudes of the poor and improving their condition in the long run. But the most striking fact about such participation is its rarity. In most of the developing nations, for some time to come, the poor are less likely to become involved in politics through this than through other patterns. Their impact on government policies will be correspondingly limited.

Conclusion:
The Routes to
Political
Participation

The Complexity of Political Participation

Political participation is a much more complex and less clear-cut phenomenon than it appears to be at first glance. It is not a single homogeneous variable. It is, rather, an umbrella encompassing many different forms of action; all of these actions are designed to influence government at some level, but they are not all related to each other, nor do they vary in the same directions or respond to the same pressures.

Crude indices, such as voting turnout, the incidence of participation in demonstrations, or party membership, can capture gross contrasts—a sudden expansion or contraction in participation within a country, or very wide differences in participation levels between two countries. But in most nations, trends in the level of political participation are usually ambiguous. Certain forms of participation expand while others contract. Previously inactive groups become more politically involved, while other groups partially withdraw. Efforts to influence the national authorities increase, but certain forms and channels of local participation atrophy. Changes in composition—the mix of forms and the types of group bases for participation—are as important, or more important, than aggregate level. The scope and intensity of political participation are also likely to vary, at times independently of each other and often in opposition to each other. Only rarely, as in times of total revolutionary upheaval, are societies likely to generate political participation that is both broad in scope and highly intense. In the context of socio-economic development, the levels, forms, and bases of political participation are shaped by the priority that elites, groups, and individuals give to political participation as a goal of development, its value in their eyes as a means to achieve other developmental goals, and the extent to which political participation is itself a by-product or consequence of development.

Political Participation as a Goal of Development

The levels, forms, and bases of political participation in a society are intimately related to the level of socio-economic development. Higher levels of participation are associated with higher levels of development. In addition, societies that are more highly developed economically and socially also tend to place greater value on political participation. In such societies, political participation comes to be viewed as inherently necessary to the effective functioning of the political system and as an inherently desirable characteristic of "man" (democratic, modern, communist) in such a society. It thus acquires value as a goal in and of itself. The ideologies and political beliefs dominant in the society stress the value of political participation. This is true, of course, for both of the major political systems found in more highly developed societies: "In totalitarian states as well as democracies, the 'good citizen' participates in public affairs. In the Soviet Union as well as the United States leaders point with pride to high rates of citizen participation and deplore apathy and indifference."[1] High levels of political participation, in forms that reflect the norms of the society, are viewed as a collective good just as high crime rates are viewed as a collective evil.

For societies in the process of changing from a rural, agrarian, less complex level of development to an urban, industrialized, highly complex level of development, changes in the levels, forms, and bases of political participation are an inherent part of the transitional process. These changes in participation are themselves selective, in that they involve particular groups attempting to achieve particular goals at particular times. They are, consequently, highly differential in the effects they have on the ability of elites, groups, and individuals to achieve their goals. In any given context, consequently, the expansion of political participation is viewed not as a generalized good for society as a whole but either as a goal competing with other goals or as a means that may be useful in achieving some goals but not others. The process of development is a process of choice for elites, groups, and individuals, and some of the most difficult of these choices concern the extent and nature of political participation by themselves and others.

Societies where elites, government, political parties, and organized groups favor the expansion of political participation as a worthy goal in and of itself are likely to be societies in which political participation is already reasonably widespread. Political participation is taken less seriously as a general goal in societies where it is less prevalent. Of course, these societies are usually at lower levels of social and economic development; although there may well be widespread agreement on the need to promote "national development," only rarely will political participation be seen as a major component of national development. Neither elites, groups, nor individuals normally stress the expansion of political participation as a general goal for their entire society or as a special goal of particular interest to them. The principal goals of political elites are to gain and hold governmental power, to promote national independence, to develop military security and domestic order, to enhance their own international prestige and that of their country, to encourage the social, regional, and cultural integration of their society, to promote economic development, and, in some instances, to push for greater social and economic equity. The principal goals of nonelite groups and individuals are to promote their own economic security and well-being, social status, and mobility opportunities; more specifically, this involves the pursuit of such goals as higher wages, job security, better working conditions, land ownership, lower rents, better housing, educational opportunities, and freedom from discrimination. Only rarely do those involved in the developmental process view the expansion of political participation as a goal of development.

Political Participation as a Means to Development

The expansion of political participation is more often seen as a way of achieving other highly valued goals in the developmental process. From this viewpoint the costs and benefits of political participation will necessarily be weighed against those of alternative means for achieving the same goal.

A political elite in control of government has more ability, but less incentive, to expand political participation than one that is not in control of government. For the latter, the mobilization of new groups into politics is an effective, although not necessarily easy, means of disrupting the status quo, changing the balance of political forces, dislodging the incumbent elite, and securing control of the government. Opposition political elites often attempt to follow this strategy, but only some are able to do so successfully. Elites in power, on the other hand, often seek to restrict or to reduce political participation in an effort to prevent challenges to their authority. They seldom seek to expand participation except in two circumstances. First, if the elite feels that it lacks a sufficient power base or constituency and is vulnerable to overthrow by the military or ouster by other means, it may attempt to mobilize a new group into politics and to organize that group as a power base in order to secure its own tenure in office. Given the resources that are available to an elite in control of the government, the probabilities are high that it will be able to carry out this strategy successfully. Second, an elite in power may feel compelled, by the competition of an opposition political elite that is attempting to mobilize new groups in politics on its side, to take parallel and comparable action to appeal to the same groups or, more likely, to mobilize other groups into politics as a counterbalance to the opposition's supporters. Outside of revolutionary situations, most significant increases in political participation during the developmental process have occurred under the auspices of elites in power and in one of these two ways.

If political elites, whether in opposition or in power, give high priority to revolutionary or nationalist goals, they also find it in their interest to expand political participation. The total destruction of the existing social, economic, and political order and its replacement with a new system requires a dramatic, far-reaching, and simultaneous expansion of both the scope and intensity of political participation. "The political essence of revolution is the rapid expansion of political consciousness and the rapid mobilization of new groups into politics at a speed which makes it impossible for existing political institutions to assimilate them. Revolution is the extreme case of the explosion of political participation."[2] This explosion is functionally necessary to secure the results of revolution. This truth is well understood by revolutionary leaders, whether they are out of power and attempting to inaugurate the revolutionary process by bringing down the existing government, or whether they are in control of the formal institutions of government and wish to carry through a revolutionary reconstruction of existing social, economic, and cultural institutions. An elite that characterizes itself as revolutionary and does not promote the expansion of political participation is defeating itself or deceiving others as to its true goals. In a similar vein, a nationalist elite aiming to displace foreign rule or influence also has to expand political participation to achieve its goal. The stronger and more intransigent the foreign power, the more extensive will be the political participation required to displace it.

Finally, the attitudes of a political elite towards political participation will often be a function of its overall political ideology and, in particular, of the extent of its commitment, revolutionary or not, to the reduction or elimination of existing class differences and to the achievement of a more egalitarian distribution of economic and social benefits. In a society in the early stages of development, if the elite is strongly committed to a radical egalitarian philosophy, it will oppose the expansion of political participation in order to minimize effective opposition to its economic and social reform measures. For, in the early stages of development, the expansion of political participation produces vocal and well-organized middle- and upper-middle-class minorities, who will naturally use their political influence on behalf of their own economic interests. As middle-class participation grows, these participants may then act effectively to obstruct the subsequent expansion of participation to the lower classes. In the political evolution of the United States, Great Britain, Sweden, and perhaps a few other countries, the transition from middle-class to working-class participation was made relatively early, although not without protest and some violence. This model, however, is seldom relevant to developing countries today. For them, the early expansion of middle-class participation along the lines of the bourgeois model is more likely to evolve into a technocratic regime that will suppress working-class participation in order to maintain middle-class control and promote economic growth. In the early stages of development, consequently, an autocratic regime that suppresses political participation and promotes economic equality through land reform and other measures may make possible, although not necessary, the subsequent expansion of political participation. In the later stages of socio-economic development, an elite committed to a more egalitarian redistribution of economic income and wealth will normally attempt to achieve those goals by expanding political participation and mobilizing the urban working class and rural peasantry into politics. These developments, however, are likely to produce a reaction from the middle classes and polarize the society. The problem then becomes, as President Allende succinctly put it in August 1973, to insure that "there will be neither a coup nor a civil war . . . " And, as his tragic fate indicates, that is not an easy goal to achieve.

The circumstances under which political elites may find the expansion of political participation useful in achieving their goals in the developmental process are limited. Such circumstances do, however, exist, and the experiences of Gandhi and Nehru, Castro, Mao, Betancourt, Frei, Peron, Cardenas, Menderes, Magsaysay, Ayub Khan, Nyerere, and others illustrate ways in which very different leaders can pursue extremely diverse social, economic, and political goals by significantly broadening political participation. These examples also illustrate the dangers and costs that such means may entail.

Social groups and individuals are, in most cases, even less likely than political elites to see political participation as a primary means of achieving their goals. Social groups, for instance, often must choose between attempting to influence government or some branch of it and alternative means such as self-help or direct action vis-a-vis other groups, without government intervention. Thus, neighborhood associations in low-income urban districts may attempt to improve their neighborhoods through self-help, through help from outside private sources, or through political action to gain help from the government. Caste associations in India, seeking to improve their members' welfare and heighten their status as a group, are faced with a comparable range of choices. In a similar manner, labor unions may deal directly with employers or attempt to put pressure on the government to intervene on their behalf. In all these cases, the groups involved must assess, in a crude and often implicit way, the costs and benefits of alternative options. Attempts to influence the government are usually of uncertain effectiveness; they are often hard to organize, and they are sometimes downright risky. Therefore, most groups normally turn first to self-help mechanisms, then to pressure on, or cooperation with, other social groups, and only lastly to attempts to influence the government. Political participation is not a weapon of first resort except when the group involved is so well-connected that success is virtually assured, or the issue is so clearly an acknowledged government responsibility that alternative means seem much less direct and promising. Under most circumstances, political participation is the weapon of last resort, when all other means of achieving group goals have been exhausted.

For the individual, the choices are to act on his own, politically or nonpolitically, or to act in cooperation with others, politically or non-politically. In general, individual action is easier than group action, and nonpolitical means are more likely to be used than political ones. Where individuals have a choice, their first resort is the most direct and immediate remedy. Unless the problem is directly caused by governmental action or can clearly be remedied only by governmental action, the individual will tend to act on his own through nongovernmental channels. This avoids both involvement with others and involvement with the government, each of which entails difficulties and risks. Individual social or economic action or, where possible, mobility (horizontal or vertical) is normally a more reliable way to achieve material betterment than involvement with others or with the government. This exit propensity is likely to be particularly prevalent among low-income individuals, since the obstacles to any collective political action by them are particularly strong. If the individual acting on his own cannot cope with the problem, he is likely, if opportunities are available, to seek help from a government official or agency, either directly or through a better-placed patron or broker. Hence the widespread prevalence of individual contacting throughout different strata in different societies. The next most plausible action, in terms of the effort and risk involved, is likely to be collective self-help by individuals who are similarly situated. Only as a last resort, in the normal course of events, will there be recourse to collective action directed at the government. This course involves the difficulties and risks of both cooperative action and governmental involvement. In addition, even where political participation is viewed as the most promising means to a desired goal, there remains a further question: how much energy is any particular person willing to invest in such action? If others with similar interests appear to be fighting his battle for him, he may rationally decide to stay out of it.[3] For the individual in a developing society, the "normal" hierarchy of choices is thus likely to be: individual nonpolitical action (exit), individual political action (contacting), collective nonpolitical action (self-help), and, lastly, collective political action.

The choices that elites, groups, and individuals make between political participation and other means of achieving goals may alternate over time. There is a certain logic to this process. If they emphasize political participation as a means towards certain goals, and if they are successful in achieving those goals, their attention is then likely to turn towards new objectives or towards old objectives that have now acquired a new priority. Political participation may not be an effective way of obtaining those new objectives. If, on the other hand, the elites, groups, or individuals fail to achieve their goals through political participation, they may turn to other means to achieve that goal or to turn to other goals that do not require political participation. Thus, while the overall process of development leads to a secular trend towards more extensive and more diversified political participation, a cyclical pattern is also likely to exist in the way actors resort to political participation as a means to achieve their goals.

Political Participation as a By-product of Development

Changes in the levels, forms, and bases of political participation are more likely to be the unintended consequence or by-product of development than the result of conscious choices by elites, groups, or individuals as either goals or means. While the relationships involved are complex and often contradictory, socio-economic development in general tends to encourage higher levels of political participation, more diverse forms of participation, more complex bases of participation (with socio-economic class of rising importance), and a higher ratio of autonomous to mobilized participation. The mechanisms at work are many; among the most important are increases in the average socio-economic level of the population and of particular groups within it, increased organizational involvement, heightened group consciousness (and, often, heightened intergroup conflict), expanded government activities impinging on more and more of the population, and the gradual acceptance among elites and nonelites of the idea of citizen responsibility and participation as a concomitant of the modern state. All of these forces are at work in both competitive and noncompetitive political systems. But the relationship between development and broadened participation is neither steady nor uniform. The level and forms of participation in a society during any period are affected by communal tensions that may be unrelated or only peripherally related to modernization, by the attitudes and policies of political elites, and by contingencies such as droughts or border disputes. These and many other factors may produce far greater or far less participation than the country's degree of social and economic modernization would lead one to expect. In general, however, political elites and other socio-economic groups that promote nation-building, state-building, economic development, socio-economic equity, national integration, and the penetration of society by government also create conditions favorable to broadened and more diversified political participation.

At the individual level, political participation is likely to be the consequence of either higher socio-economic status or heightened identification with a particular socio-economic or communal group. Development increases the absolute and relative number of educated middle-class people in a society. These people feel better able to influence the government; they perceive more clearly its actual or potential relevance to their own interests; and they are more likely to believe that it is a citizen's duty to participate in politics. When high-status people withdraw from politics, it is usually because they feel ineffective. Sometimes the very process of extending participation to previously inactive and—Mexico parochial groups alters the balance of power and the issues and values of politics in ways that alienate educated and cosmopolitan elites. Greater economic independence, even when associated with only very modest economic and social status, also seems to promote participation; for example, land ownership, home ownership (or its functional equivalent, urban squatting that is accepted by the authorities), and self-employed status, if it is above the marginal level of petty vendor or odd-job man.

Still more powerful than socio-economic status in explaining (and increasing) political participation is organizational involvement. In the course of development, social and economic organizations of all types proliferate, some based on new interests and identifications, others reflecting pre-existing communal (tribal, religious, regional, caste) loyalties, which are often altered and heightened by modernization itself. Such organizations may coincide with or cut across class and status lines. High-status people everywhere are likely to be involved in organizations, which reinforces the effects of status in encouraging their political participation. Low-status people are likely to become involved in organizations if they have a sense of ethnicity, neighborhood, or class. Among poor people, such consciousness is likely to spring from conflict—with other social groups or with the authorities—and from an insulation against competing affiliations and loyalties.

Political participation, as a by-product, feeds back to and constrains the political choices of elites and groups. As development proceeds, participation becomes increasingly costly to suppress, at least among socially mobilized segments of the population. Therefore, elites are constrained to channel rather than to suppress participation, that is, to control its forms and guide the selection of issues. As some groups become politically active, others are under pressure to do likewise in order to protect their relative positions. This process of defensive and imitative group mobilization is particularly characteristic of ethnically divided societies.

Political participation expands both because more people become less poor and because more people become more politically conscious. Political parties must reflect these trends and must eventually mobilize and organize those who have achieved higher socio-economic status and those who have developed higher levels of group consciousness. There is, however, no guarantee that the least privileged members of a society will find either a political voice or political champions. Nor is there any guarantee that the expansion of political participation will not intensify social and political conflict and give rise to widespread political instability. Experience suggests that in the absence of a highly developed party system, whether single party or competitive, such instability is likely to be the consequence of socio-economic development.[4]

The "Cascading Effect" of Participation Choices

Over time, the nature and level of political participation in a society are shaped by the processes of socio-economic development. In the early phases of modernization, a conflict exists between the goals of socio-economic equity and political participation, while in the later stages there is a conflict between economic growth and political participation. While some countries have been able to balance and contain these conflicting goals, in most developing countries the dominant political elites must choose among the various goals and means. The choices made by these elites create, in turn, the context for the choices made by those at lower levels. Elite choices as to the relative priority of economic growth, socio-economic equity, political stability, and other goals substantially affect the costs and benefits to groups and individuals of resorting to political participation as either a goal or a means. Similarly, group choices constrain individual behavior; whatever his social background, an individual is much more likely to participate if the group context encourages him to do so. Indeed, he may only be able to participate if the group provides support and guidance. Because of this "cascading effect," elite choices and attitudes toward participation and other goals are the most powerful determinants of the extent and nature of political participation in a society at any given time, and the group context in which the individual functions is normally more important than his particular social background characteristics in determining the scope and nature of his participation.

This point is well illustrated by the case of neighborhood associations. The fact that associations develop in some neighborhoods and not in others can be partly explained in terms of the nature of the residents' tenure, the size of the neighborhoods, the presence or absence of clear-cut boundaries, the homogeneity or heterogeneity of the residents, and internal political factors such as leadership and factionalism. But these factors are dwarfed by the broader political context, at least in determining the associations' political activities. In Chile, the governments of both Frei and Allende actively promoted politically participant neighborhood associations. In the early 1970s, Peru also worked with and through such associations, although they were treated less as independent entities than as committees for cooperation with government programs. Castro's Cuba has required the formation of neighborhood committees, which are clearly arms of the regime but also serve certain modest political participation functions. While Venezuela and Mexico tolerate associations and often respond to specific associations' petitions, they do not particularly promote them. Brazil has been clearly hostile. These various elite decisions are as important, or more important, than strictly local conditions in determining the number and the nature of neighborhood associations.

Similarly, at the individual level, if there is an association in a particular neighborhood, some will choose to join and others will abstain. The incidence of membership can be partly explained by individual characteristics such as education, migrant status, membership in other voluntary organizations, and certain attitudes. But in the city as a whole, the number of people who engage in this form of political participation is first and foremost determined by the incidence and nature of the associations themselves. If we turn from neighborhood associations to more familiar vehicles for participation, such as labor unions, peasant syndicates, and political parties, it becomes even more obvious that government policies and opposition elite strategies have a cascading impact, through groups and organizations, on individual participation.

The cascading effect of elite choices is so obvious that it would not bear mentioning, except that in the past two decades scholarship on political participation has tended to stress economic and social determinants to the virtual exclusion of the political context. At the micro level, surveys on individual participation have intensively explored individual attributes and attitudes. More recently, studies have also taken into account the social context of neighborhood or factory. But the political context, as it impinges on the individual—his real opportunities for participation—are often ignored or studied only obliquely, through broad questions on attitudes toward the political system in general. At the macro level, too, cross-national studies of the extent and nature of political participation have focused on those economic and social factors for which comparable data are available for different countries, and have abstracted these factors from non-comparable political factors.

These studies have greatly enhanced our understanding of the mechanisms that produce a secular trend toward expanded political participation. But they are much less helpful in explaining the tremendous variations that exist in the forms, bases, and patterns of participation. It is precisely here that the notion of the cascading impact of elite choices may be most helpful. The economic and social forces feeding the expansion of political participation seem to be global and inexorable in the long run. But sudden short-term fluctuations in partici-

Conclusion: The Routes to Political Participation

pation levels are usually the direct results of elite actions. The forms and patterns assumed by expanding political participation are malleable; they can be molded and formed into a wide range of systems, differing so sharply that what is viewed as participation in one society is not even recognized by that label in another. These differences in the forms, bases, and overall patterns of participation, while influenced by general social and economic trends, are primarily the product of the decisions of political elites.

Notes

1. Introduction

1. Address to the Board of Governors of the World Bank Group, International Bank for Reconstruction and Development, Washington, D.C., Sept. 25, 1972, p. 19.

2. *Ibid.,* p. 20.

3. See Chapter 1, pp. 4-7, for a fuller discussion of this definition.

4. Myron Weiner, "Political Participation: Crisis of the Political Process," in Leonard Binder et al., *Crises and Sequences in Political Development* (Princeton: Princeton University Press, 1971), p. 164.

5. Norman H. Nie and Sidney Verba, "Political Participation," in Fred Greenstein and Nelson Polsby (eds.), *Handbook of Political Science* (Reading, Mass.: Addison-Wesley, 1975), Vol. III, p. 2.

6. Data sources are as follows: (1) Charles Lewis Taylor and Michael C. Hudson, *World Handbook of Political and Social Indicators,* 2nd ed. (New Haven: Yale University Press, 1972), pp. 54-56; (2) Nie and Verba, "Political Participation," in Greenstein and Polsby (eds.), *Handbook of Political Science,* p. 29; (3) Norman H. Nie, G. Bingham Powell, Jr., and Kenneth Prewitt, "Social Structure and Political Participation: Developmental Relationships, II," *American Political Science Review,* 63 (Sept. 1969), p. 824.

7. See Sidney Verba, Norman H. Nie, and Jae-On Kim, *The Modes of Democratic Participation: A Cross-National Comparison* (Beverly Hills, Calif.: Sage Publications, 1971), pp. 41-43, 57-59.

8. *Ibid.,* pp. 26-44.

9. For a useful summary and analysis of political violence in terms of theories of relative deprivation, see Ted Robert Gurr, *Why Men Rebel* (Princeton: Princeton University Press, 1970). For a brief, general discussion of violence in relation to development, see Samuel P. Huntington, "Civil Violence and the Process of Development," in International Institute of Strategic Studies, *Civil Violence and the International System: Part II, Violence and International Security* (Adelphi Paper No. 83, December 1971), pp. 1-15.

2. Goals and Choices

1. *An International Economy* (New York: Harper, 1956), p. 133.

2. Address, Montreal, Quebec, May 18, 1966.

3. S. M. Lipset, "Some Social Requisites of Democracy: Economic Development and Political Legitimacy," *American Political Science Review,* 52 (March 1959), pp. 69ff.; Daniel Lerner, *The Passing of Traditional Society* (Glencoe, Ill.: The Free Press, 1958).

4. For summaries of the evidence on this point, see Samuel P. Huntington, *Political Order in Changing Societies* (New Haven: Yale University Press, 1968), pp. 39-59, and "Civil Violence and the Process of Development," in International Institute of Strategic Studies, *Civil Violence and the International System: Part II, Violence and International Security.* (Adelphi Paper No. 83, December, 1971), pp. 1-15.

5. Irma Adelman, "Summary, Conclusions, and Recommendations," Part I, Final Report, Grant AID/csd/2236. Northwestern University, February 12, 1971, p. 6. Some aspects of the relation between economic growth and the concentration of wealth in Pakistan are touched upon in Shahid Javed Burki, "Social Groups and Development: A Case Study of Pakistan" (Unpublished manuscript, Harvard Center for International Affairs, 1972), chapter 7.

6. For a brilliant critique of the economic development-political democracy literature, see Jonathan Sunshine, "The Economic Basis and Consequences of Democracy: The Need to Study the Time Dimension" (Unpublished paper, American Political Science Association, Annual Meeting, Washington, D.C., September 1972).

7. Henry Bienen, *Kenya: The Politics of Participation and Control* (Princeton: Princeton University Press, 1974), pp. 4-5.

8. *Ibid.,* p. 45.

9. Wayne A. Cornelius, "Urbanization and Political Demand-Making," *American Political Science Review,* 68 (Sept. 1974), pp. 1139-40; Daniel Goldrich, Raymond B. Pratt, and C. R. Schuller, *The Political Integration of Lower-Class Urban Settlements in Chile and Peru* (St. Louis, Mo.: Washington University Social Science Institute, Studies in Comparative International Development, Vol. III, No. 1, 1967-68), pp. 10-14.

10. Lester W. Milbrath, "Political Participation in the States," in Herbert Jacob and Kenneth N. Vines (eds.), *Politics in the American States* (Boston: Little, Brown and Co., 1965), pp. 40-43.

11. Peter McDonough, "Electoral Competition and Participation in India: A Test of Huntington's Hypothesis," *Comparative Politics,* 4 (October 1971), pp. 77-87.

12. Michael Brower, "Voting Patterns in Recent Colombian Elections" (Unpublished paper, Harvard University, Center for International Affairs, September 1971).

13. Quoted in Irwin Ross, "From Ataturk to Gursal: What Went Wrong in Turkey?" *New Leader,* 43, no. 47 (1960), pp. 14-18.

14. Burki, "Social Groups and Development," p. 2-2.

15. *Ibid.,* pp. 2-34 - 2-35, 3-15, 6-38ff.

16. *Ibid.,* Chapter 10, passim.

17. Jeffrey Race, *War Comes to Long An* (Berkeley: University of California Press, 1972), p. 160.

18. For an analysis of these trends in the land reform program, see Kevin Middlebrook, "Land for the Tiller: Political Participation and the Peruvian Military's Agrarian Reform" (Honors thesis, Harvard College, 1972).

19. For suggestive hypotheses on this shift in leadership, see John H. Kautsky, "Revolutionary and Managerial Elites in Modernizing Regimes," *Comparative Politics,* 1 (July 1969), pp. 441-67.

20. Cornelius, "Urbanization and Political Demand-Making," pp. 1131-33.

21. Bienen, *Kenya,* pp. 49-57.

22. John D. Montgomery, "Allocation of Authority in Land Reform Programs: A Comparative Study of Administrative Processes and Outputs," *Administrative Science Quarterly,* 17 (March 1972), pp. 62-75.

3. Development, Equality, and Participation

1. Daniel Lerner, *The Passing of Traditional Society* (Glencoe, Ill.: The Free Press, 1958), p. 50.

2. Norman H. Nie, G. Bingham Powell, Jr., and Kenneth Prewitt, "Social Structure and Political Participation: Developmental Relationships, Part I," *American Political Science Review,* 63 (June 1969), p. 369.

3. Lester W. Milbrath, *Political Participation* (Chicago: Rand McNally, 1965), p. 120; Thomas R. Dye, *Politics, Economics and the Public* (Chicago: Rand McNally, 1966), p. 267.

4. Ergun Özbudun, "Social Change and Political Participation in Turkey" (Unpublished manuscript, Harvard University, Center for International Affairs, 1973), p. 3-25.

5. Ronald D. Brunner and Garry D. Brewer, *Organized Complexity: Empirical Theories of Political Development* (New York: The Free Press, 1971), pp. 10-11.

6. See Henry Bienen, *Kenya: The Politics of Participation and Control* (Princeton: Princeton University Press, 1974), pp. 87ff.; Nelson M. Kasfir, "Controlling Ethnicity in Ugandan Politics: Departicipation as a Strategy for Political Development in Africa" (Ph.D. thesis, Harvard University, 1972), especially chapter 8.

7. Marc Howard Ross, "Urbanization and Political Participation: The Effect of Increasing Scale in Nairobi" (Paper presented to Annual Meeting,

African Studies Association, Boston, 1970); Bienen, *Kenya,* pp. 14-15.

8. Sidney Tarrow, "The Urban-Rural Cleavage in Political Involvement: The Case of France," *American Political Science Review,* 65 (June 1971), pp. 344-45; Özbudun, "Social Change and Political Participation," pp. 5-1 - 5-5; Hung-Chao Tai, *Land Reform and Politics* (Berkeley: The University of California Press, 1974), pp. 352-53, 357.

9. John D. Powell, "Peasants in Politics" (Unpublished manuscript, Harvard University, Center for International Affairs, 1972), pp. 4-5 - 4-8.

10. Alex Inkeles, "Participant Citizenship in Six Developing Countries," *American Political Science Review,* 63 (December 1969), pp. 1132-37.

11. M. Lal Goel, "The Relevance of Education for Political Participation in a Developing Society," *Comparative Political Studies,* 3 (October, 1970), p. 340.

12. Nie et al., *American Political Science Review,* 63 (June 1969), pp. 365-69.

13. See Herbert Tingsten, *Political Behavior* (Totowa, N.J.: Bedminster Press, 1963), pp. 10ff.; Stein Rokkan, "Electoral Mobilization, Party Competition, and National Intergration," in Joseph LaPalombara and Myron Weiner (eds.), *Political Parties and Political Development* (Princeton: Princeton University Press, 1966), pp. 238-49; John Field, remarks, "Panel Discussion of Elections and Political Development in Turkey, India, and Colombia," Harvard-MIT Joint Seminar on Political Development, October 27, 1971.

14. See Jorge Domínguez, "Social Mobilization, Traditional Political Participation, and Government Response in Early 19th Century Spanish America" (Ph.D. thesis, Harvard University, 1972).

15. Özbudun, "Social Change and Political Participation," p. 4-6.

16. See Albert Hirschman, *Exit, Voice, and Loyalty* (Cambridge: Harvard University Press, 1970), passim.

17. John M. Orbell and Toru Uno, "A Theory of Neighborhood Problem-Solving: Political Action vs. Residential Mobility," *American Political Science Review,* 66 (June 1972), p. 484. For a more extended analysis of this relationship, see also Chapter 4 of this book.

18. Powell, "Peasants in Politics," pp. 4-9ff.

19. Özbudun, "Social Change and Political Participation," pp. 7-8 - 7-11, 7-36.

20. *Ibid.,* pp. 5-2 - 5-4.

21. Powell, "Peasants in Politics," pp. 4-15 - 4-16.

22. *Ibid.,* pp. 4-16, 4-53 - 4-56.

23. *Ibid.,* pp. 4-23ff., 4-33ff.

24. Francine R. Frankel and Karl von Vorys, *The Political Challenge of the Green Revolution: Shifting Patterns of Peasant Participation in India and Pakistan* (University of Pennsylvania, Department of Political Science, August 10, 1971), mimeo, p. 45.

25. See Joji Watanuki, "Japanese Politics in Flux," in James W. Morley

(ed.), *Prologue to the Future* (Lexington, Mass.: D.C. Heath, 1974), pp. 77-79.

26. Wayne A. Cornelius, "A Structural Analysis of Urban Caciquismo in Mexico," *Urban Anthropology*, 1 (Fall 1972), pp. 248-51.

27. Michael Brower, "Voting Patterns in Recent Colombian Presidential Elections" (Unpublished paper, Harvard Center for International Affairs, September 30, 1971).

28. Robert H. Dix, "Political Oppositions Under the Colombian National Front," in R.A. Berry, Ronald Hellman, and Mauricio Solaun (eds.), *Coalition Government in Colombia* (New York: Cyrco Press, 1976).

29. Ozbudun, "Social Change and Political Participation," pp. 6-6ff.

30. Özbudun, "The Political Behavior of the Urban Poor in Turkey" (Unpublished paper, University of Ankara, 1975), p. 12.

31. Bruce M. Russett, "Inequality and Instability: The Relaton of Land Tenure and Politics," *World Politics,* 16 (April 1964), pp. 442-54. See also Robert A. Dahl, *Polyarchy: Participation and Opposition* (New Haven: Yale University Press, 1971), chapters 4, 6.

32. Phillips Cutright, "Inequality: A Cross-National Analysis," *American Sociological Review*, 32 (August 1967), pp. 562ff.

33. Jonathan Sunshine, "Economic Causes and Consequences of Democracy: A Study in Historical Statistics of the European and European-Populated English-Speaking Countries" (Ph.D. thesis, Columbia University, 1972).

34. For another discussion of this problem in terms of the differences between "education-driven" and "pecking-order" models with respect to political efficacy, see Philip E. Converse, "Change in the American Electorate," in Angus Campbell and Philip E. Converse (eds.), *The Human Meaning of Social Change* (New York: Russell Sage Foundation, 1972), pp. 325-29.

35. Robert R. Alford and Eugene C. Lee, "Voting Turnout in American Cities," *American Political Science Review*, 62 (September 1968), p. 811.

36. Powell, "Peasants in Politics," p. 4-9.

37. Cutright, "Inequality," pp. 562ff.

38. Phillips Cutright, "Political Structure, Economic Development, and National Social Security Programs," *American Journal of Sociology*, 70 (March 1965), 537ff.

39. Irma Adelman, "Summary, Conclusions, and Recommendations," Part I, Final Report, Grand AID/csd/2236. Northwestern University, February 12, 1971, p. 7.

40. Bienen, *Kenya*, pp. 104, 112.

41. Özbudun, "Social Change and Political Participation," p. 4-35 (Footnotes omitted).

42. *Ibid.*, p. 4-36.

43. Wayne A. Cornelius, "Urbanization and Political Demand-Making: Political Participation Among the Migrant Poor in Latin American Cities," *American Political Science Review*, 68 (September 1974), pp. 1137-38.

44. The evidence on this point is set forth at length in Samuel P. Huntington, *Political Order in Changing Societies* (New Haven: Yale University Press, 1968), pp. 380-96, and Tai, *Land Reform and Politics,* passim.

45. Sidney Verba and Norman H. Nie, *Participation in America: Political Democracy and Social Equality* (New York: Harper & Row, 1972), pp. 509-18.

4. Mobility, Organization, and Participation

1. Norman H. Nie, G. Bingham Powell, and Kenneth Prewitt, "Social Structure and Political Participation: Developmental Relationships, Part I," *American Political Science Review*, 63 (June 1968), pp. 370-74.

2. Alex Inkeles, "Participant Citizenship in Six Developing Countries," *American Political Science Review*, 63 (December 1969), pp. 1135-37; Gabriel Almond and Sidney Verba, *The Civic Culture* (Boston: Little Brown, 1965), pp. 315-16; Sidney Verba, Norman H. Nie, and Jae-On Kim, *The Modes of Democratic Participation: A Cross-National Comparison* (Beverly Hills, Calif.: Sage Publications, 1971), pp. 55-77.

3. See Robert A. Dahl, *Who Governs?* (New Haven: Yale University Press, 1961), p. 291.

4. Lester W. Milbrath, *Political Participation* (Chicago: Rand McNally, 1966), pp. 61-63.

5. Jesse F. Marquette, "Social Mobilization and the Philippine Political System," *Comparative Political Studies*, 4 (October 1971), p. 346.

6. Alvin Rabushka, "A Note on Overseas Chinese Political Participation in Urban Malaya," *American Political Science Review*, 64 (March 1970), p. 178.

7. M. Lal Goel, "The Relevance of Education for Political Participation in a Developing Society," *Comparative Political Studies*, 3 (October 1970), pp. 333-46.

8. *Ibid.*, p. 345.

9. See Samuel P. Huntington, *Political Order in Changing Societies* (New Haven: Yale University Press, 1968), chapter 4.

10. Robert R. Alford and Harry M. Scoble, "Sources of Local Political Involvement," *American Political Science Review*, 62 (December 1968), p. 1205.

11. John R. Mathieson and John D. Powell, "Participation and Efficacy: Aspects of Peasant Involvement in Political Mobilization," *Comparative Politics*, 4 (April 1972), pp. 312-13.

12. J. C. Van Es and Robert L. Whittenbarger, "Farm Ownership, Political Participation, and Other Social Participation in Central Brazil" (University of Wisconsin Land Tenure Center, LTC Paper No. 50, July 1968), p. 17.

13. David Collier, "Squatter Settlement Formation and the Politics of Cooptation in Peru," (Ph.D. thesis, University of Chicago, 1971) pp. 140-42; Ergun Özbudun, "Social Change and Political Participation in Turkey" (Un-

published manuscript, Harvard University, Center for International Affairs, 1973) p. 8-15.

14. Lester Salamon, "Protest, Politics, and Modernization in the American South: Mississippi as a 'Developing Society' " (Ph.D. thesis, Harvard University, 1972), pp. 465, 661-62, 674-75.

15. Robert A. Dahl, *Polyarchy: Participation and Opposition* (New Haven: Yale University Press, 1971), pp. 53-56.

16. Wayne A. Cornelius, "Urbanization and Political Demand-Making: Political Participation Among the Migrant Poor in Latin American Cities," *American Political Science Review,* 68 (September 1974), p. 1134.

17. Nie, *et al.*, "Social Structure and Political Participation," p. 368; William Erbe, "Social Involvement and Political Activity: A Replication and Elaboration," *American Sociological Review*, 29 (April 1964), pp. 198-215; Seymour Martin Lipset, *Political Man* (New York: Doubleday, 1960), pp. 193-98.

18. Lipset, *Political Man*, p. 195; Erbe, "Social Involvement and Political Activity," p. 209. See also Anthony M. Orum, "A Reappraisal of the Social and Political Participation of Negroes," *American Journal of Sociology*, 72 (July 1966), p. 35.

19. Stein Rokkan, *Citizens, Elections, Parties* (Oslo: Universitaetsforlaget, 1970), pp. 383-84.

20. Nie, *et al.*, "Social Structure and Political Participation," p. 364.

21. *Ibid.*, p. 813.

22. Mathiason and Powell, "Participation and Efficacy," pp. 317-21.

23. Wayne A. Cornelius, *Politics and the Migrant Poor in Mexico City* (Stanford, Calif.: Stanford University Press, 1975), pp. 73-108, 133-34.

24. Cornelius, "Urbanization and Political Demand-Making," p. 1134.

25. Marvin E. Olsen, "Social and Political Participation of Blacks," *American Sociological Review*, 35 (August 1970), pp. 695-96.

26. Sidney Verba and Norman H. Nie, *Participation in America: Political Democracy and Social Equality* (New York: Harper & Row, 1972), pp. 157-62.

27. Alessandro Pizzorno, "An Introduction to the Theory of Political Participation," *Social Science Information*, 9 (1970), p. 45.

28. Wayne A. Cornelius, "The Cityward Movement: Some Political Implications," *Proceedings of the Academy of Political Science,* 30 (August 1972), pp. 35-36.

29. Cornelius, *Politics and the Migrant Poor,* p. 112.

30. John D. Powell, "Peasants in Politics" (Unpublished manuscript, Harvard University, Center for International Affairs, 1972), pp. 3-48.

31. Cornelius, *Politics and the Migrant Poor,* p. 134.

32. Gerald W. Johnson, "Research Note on Political Correlation of Voter Participation: A Deviant Case Analysis," *American Political Science Review*, 65 (September 1971), p. 772.

33. Cornelius, *Politics and the Migrant Poor,* pp. 103-04, 124, 127-28.

34. Robert E. Lane, *Political Life: Why People Get Involved in Politics* (Glencoe, Ill.: Free Press, 1959), pp. 236-43.

35. Lipset, *Political Man,* pp. 193-94.

36. Herbert Tingsten, *Political Behavior* (Totowa, N.J.: Bedminister Press, 1965), p. 230, pp. 126-27; Milbrath, *Political Participation,* pp. 97-98, 119; Lipset, *Political Man,* pp. 206-7.

37. Lane, *Political Life,* pp. 263-64.

38. Powell, "Peasants in Politics," pp. 4-9ff.

39. Cornelius, *Politics and the Migrant Poor,* p. 130.

40. Erik Allardt and Kettil Brunn, "Characteristics of the Finnish Non-Voter," *Westermarck Society Transactions,* 3 (1956), p. 60.

41. Rokkan, *Citizens, Elections, Parties,* p. 380.

42. Lipset, *Political Man,* p. 197.

43. Powell, "Peasants in Politics," p. 4-6.

44. Henry A. Landsberger, "Class Mobility and Working Class and Peasant Movements: The Partial Integration of Two Conceptual Fields" (Paper presented to 1970 Annual Meeting, American Sociological Association, Washington, D.C., August-September 1970), especially pp. 23-29.

45. Albert Hirschman, *Exit, Voice, and Loyalty: Responses to Decline in Firms, Organizations, and States* (Cambridge: Harvard University Press, 1970). For another general discussion, see Samuel P. Huntington, "Migration, Politics, and Peasant Responses to Modernization" (Unpublished paper, Harvard University, Center for International Affairs, January 1971).

46. Lane, *Political Life,* pp. 254-55.

47. Henry Bienen, *Kenya: The Politics of Participation and Control* (Princeton: Princeton University Press, 1974), pp. 119-121; Özbudun, "Social Change and Political Participation," pp. 3-26ff.

48. Lipset, *Political Man,* p. 206.

49. Olsen, "Social and Political Participation of Blacks," pp. 692-93; Orum, "A Reappraisal," p. 36.

50. John M. Orbell and Toru Uno, "A Theory of Neighborhood Problem-Solving: Political Action vs. Residential Mobility," *American Political Science Review,* 66 (June 1972), pp. 478-86.

51. Özbudun, "Social Change and Political Participation," pp. 8-14 - 8-19.

52. J.S. MacDonald, "Agricultural Organization, Migration and Labour Militancy in Rural Italy," *Economic History Review,* 16 (1963-64), pp. 61-75.

53. John D. Powell, *Political Mobilization of the Venezuelan Peasant* (Cambridge: Harvard University Press, 1971), chapter 10.

54. MacDonald, "Agricultural Organization, Migration and Labour Militancy in Rural Italy," pp. 68, 70.

55. Joan M. Nelson, "Causes and Consequences of Temporary Versus Permanent Migration," *Economic Development and Cultural Change,* forthcoming, 1976.

56. *Ibid.*
57. Cornelius, *Politics and the Migrant Poor,* pp. 127-28.
58. Cornelius, "Cityward Movement," p. 34.
59. Cornelius, "Urbanization and Political Demand-Making," pp. 1141-1143. See also Chapter 5 of this book.
60. Burki, "Social Groups and Development," p. 9-27.
61. Özbudun, "Social Change and Political Participation," pp. 8-27 - 8-28; Cornelius, "Cityward Movement," pp. 30-31.
62. Cornelius, *Politics and the Migrant Poor,* p. 132; see also Chapter 5 of this book.
63. Bienen, *Kenya,* p. 119.
64. Huntington, *Political Order in Changing Societies,* p. 283.
65. Cornelius, "Cityward Movement," p. 39.
66. *Ibid.,* pp. 39-40.
67. Özbudun, "Social Change and Political Participation," p. 8-20.
68. *Ibid.,* p. 8-21.

5. Political Participation by the Poor

1. For a detailed discussion of the varying life circumstances of different economic categories of peasants, see John D. Powell, "Peasants in Politics " (Unpublished manuscript, Harvard University, Center for International Affairs, 1972), chapters 2 and 3.

2. See Joan M. Nelson, *Migrants, Urban Poverty, and Instability in New Nations* (Cambridge, Mass.: Harvard University, Center for International Affairs, Occasional Paper Number 22, September 1969), p. 35, for a brief discussion of definitional problems relating to the concept of the "urban poor." For an intriguing discussion of how poor people get by in the cities of developing nations, see Keith Hart, "Informal Income Opportunities and the Structure of Urban Employment in Ghana," *Journal of Modern African Studies,* 11 (March 1973), pp. 61-89. For discussions of the difficulty of defining unemployment in developing nations, and therefore the inadvisability of equating unemployment or underemployment with the problem of poverty, see W. F. Maunder, *Employment in an Underdeveloped Area: A Sample Survey of Kingston, Jamaica* (New Haven: Yale University Press, 1960), especially chapter 2; David Turnham, *The Unemployment Problem in Less Developed Countries* (Paris: OECD, June 1970).

3. See the article by Gerrit Huizer, "Resistance to Change and Radical Peasant Mobilization: Foster and Erasmus Reconsidered," *Human Organization,* 29 (Winter 1970), pp. 303-312; and the replies of Foster and Erasmus in the same journal. For a somewhat parallel critique of the notion of the culture of poverty in urban settings, see Charles A. Valentine, *Culture and Poverty* (Chicago: University of Chicago Press, 1968).

4. See Joan M. Nelson, "Sojourners versus New Urbanites: Causes and Consequences of Temporary versus Permanent Cityward Migration in Developing Nations," *Economic Development and Cultural Change* (in press, mid-1976).

5. Our analysis of patterns most likely to engage the poor partly parallels the more general "paths to politics" identified by Sidney Verba, Kenneth Nie, and Jae-on Kim, *The Modes of Democratic Participation* (Beverly Hills, Calif.: Sage Professional Papers, Comparative Politics Series No. 01-013, 1971). Drawing on cross-national survey data, their paths refer mostly to individual motivations, while the patterns we discuss are syndromes of goals, leadership, scale, and tactics. Verba and his associates identify three paths other than socio-economic status that may stimulate political participation: highly perceived personal relevance of government, group consciousness, and partisan mobilization. Personal relevance, they suggest, leads to particularized contacting. In our analysis it may also lead to small special interest groups. Group consciousness is obviously the path to politics operative in ethnic parties and nationalist movements. In principle, such consciousness might also apply to class-oriented parties, but in practice class consciousness is rare among the poor in developing nations. Instead, partisan mobilization seems to us to be a more likely path to participation by some of the poor in parties that are partly poor-oriented. But agencies other than parties may also seek to mobilize the poor. In some Latin American countries, for example, the Church has been effective in organizing rural poor into peasant unions or cooperatives. The term "*partisan* mobilization" therefore is too restricted for the pattern we describe. One category in our list that has no parallel in Verba and his associates' analysis is mobilized participation. This is to be expected, since strictly speaking, voting or otherwise acting to please or placate a leader is not political participation as Verba and his colleagues define the term. Our reasons for including mobilized participation in our analysis were discussed in Chapter 1.

6. Many anthropological studies of African tribes discuss traditional chiefs and their relationships to their followers. For traditional chiefs in urban settings, see Peter C.W. Gutkind, "African Urban Chiefs," in Paul Meadows and Ephraim H. Mizruchi (eds.), *Urbanism, Urbanization and Change* (Reading, Mass.: Addison-Wesley, 1969), pp. 457-469; also Abner Cohen, *Custom and Politics in Urban Africa* (Berkeley: Univ. of California Press, 1969), passim.

7. For good discussions of patron-client networks and their political implications, see John D. Powell, "Peasant Society and Clientelist Politics," *American Political Science Review*, 64 (June 1970), pp. 411-26; Rene Lemarchand, "Political Clientelism and Ethnicity in Tropical Africa: Competing Solidarities in Nation-Building," *American Political Science Review*, 65 (March 1972), pp. 68-90; James C. Scott, "Patron-Client Politics and Political Change in Southeast Asia," *American Political Science Review*, 65 (March 1972), pp. 91-113; Alex Weingrod, "Patrons, Patronage, and Political Parties," *Comparative Studies in*

Society and History, 10 (1967-68), pp. 377-400; and Robert Kaufman, "The Patron-Client Concept and Macro-Politics: Prospects and Problems," *Comparative Studies in Society and History,* 16 (June 1974), pp. 284-308.

8. Weingrod, "Patrons," p. 391.

9. John R. Mathiason and John D. Powell, "Participation and Efficacy: Aspects of Peasant Involvement in Political Mobilization," *Comparative Politics*, 4 (Spring 1972), p. 310.

10. See, for example, Jorge Giusti, "Organizational Characteristics of the Latin American Urban Marginal Settler," *International Journal of Politics*, 1 (1971), p. 81; Andrew Pearse, "Algunas Caracteristicas de la Urbanizacion en Rio de Janeiro," United Nations Economic and Social Council, Seminar on Problems of Urbanization in Latin America, E/CN. 12/URB/17, 1959, pp. 12-13.

11. See, for example, Bryan Roberts, "Politics in a Neighborhood of Guatemala City," *Sociology,* 2 (May 1968), pp. 186-87 and "The Social Organization of Low-Income Urban Families," in Richard N. Adams, *Crucifixion by Power* (Austin, Texas: University of Texas Press, 1970), pp. 481, 505-6. For a parallel argument in the African context, see J. C. Mitchell, "Theoretical Orientations in African Urban Studies," in Michael Banton (ed.), *The Social Anthropology of Complex Societies* (New York: Barnes and Noble, 1966).

12. See, for example, Aprodicio Laquian, *The City in Nation-Building* (Manila: College of Public Administration, University of the Philippines, 1966), pp. 97, 135.

13. For a discussion of urban political machines in developing countries see James C. Scott, "Corruption, Machine Politics, and Political Change," *American Political Science Review*, 63 (December 1969), pp. 1142-58.

14. Aristide Zolberg, *One-Party Government in the Ivory Coast* (Princeton: Princeton University Press, 1964), p. 337.

15. James C. Scott, "Corruption, Machine Politics, and Political Change," p. 1158.

16. See, for example, the description of the appeal of the political machine to European immigrants in U.S. cities in the late nineteenth and early twentieth centuries, in Oscar Handlin, *The Uprooted* (Boston: Little, Brown, 1951), pp. 201-2, 213.

17. C. S. Whitaker, Jr., *The Politics of Tradition: Continuity and Change in Northern Nigeria 1946-66* (Princeton: Princeton University Press, 1970), pp. 374-75.

18. See, for example, Wayne A. Cornelius, "A Structural Analysis of Urban Caciquismo in Mexico," in Robert Kern (ed.), *The Caciques* (Albuquerque, New Mexico, University of New Mexico Press, 1973), p. 146.

19. Verba, Ahmed, and Bhatt, *Caste, Race, and Politics: A Comparative Study of India and the United States* (Beverly Hills, Calif.: Sage, 1971), Table 34, p. 165.

20. Wayne A. Cornelius, "Urbanization and Political Demand-Making: Political Participation among the Migrant Poor in Latin American Cities," *American Political Science Review,* 68 (September 1974), p. 1136.

21. Joan M. Nelson, "Migration, Integration of Migrants and the Problem of Squatter Settlements in Seoul, Korea" (Report on a Field Study for the Smithsonian Institution, mimeographed, July 1972), p. 24.

22. *Ibid.,* p. 20.

23. Lisa R. Peattie, *The View from the Barrio* (Ann Arbor: University of Michigan Press, 1968), chapter 7, "The Great Sewer Controversy." On use of radio and press by local associations to generate support, see also Talton Ray, *The Politics of the Barrios of Venzuela* (Berkeley, Calif.: University of California Press, 1969), pp. 96-97.

24. Joan M. Nelson, unpublished field notes from Santiago, Chile, July 1969; Anthony and Elizabeth Leeds, "Favelas and Polity: The Continuity of the Structure of Social Control," LADAC Occasional Papers, Series 2, No. 5 (Austin, Texas: Institute of Latin American Studies, University of Texas, 1972), pp. 18-19 of draft version; Ray, *Politics of the Barrios,* chapter 7.

25. See, for example, Michael Lipsky and Margaret Levi, "Community Organization as a Political Resource: The Case of Housing" (paper prepared for the American Political Science Association Conference, September 1970); James Q. Wilson, "The Strategy of Protest: Problems of Negro Civic Action," *Journal of Conflict Resolution,* 5 (September 1969), pp. 291-303; Mayer N. Zald and Robert Ash, "Social Movement Organization: Growth, Decay, and Change," in Joseph R. Gusfield (ed.), *Protest, Reform, and Revolt* (New York: Wiley, 1970); Lee Rainwater, "Neighborhood Action and Lower Class Life Styles," in John B. Turner (ed.), *Neighborhood Organization for Community Action* (New York: National Association of Social Workers, 1968); Saul Alinsky, *Reveille for Radicals* (New York: Random House, 1969).

26. For empirical evidence on this point, see Alejandro Portes, "Rationality in the Slum: An Essay on Interpretive Sociology," *Comparative Studies in Society and History,* 14 (June 1972), pp. 273-74, especially table 1.

27. Elizabeth and Anthony Leeds, "Favelas and Polity," pp. 48-49 of draft version.

28. *Ibid.*

29. See John Powell's account of the detailed regulations imposed on Venezuelan peasant syndicates as a control device, in *Political Mobilization of the Venezuelan Peasant* (Cambridge, Mass.: Harvard University Press, 1971), pp. 59-60.

30. Peattie, *View from the Barrio,* chapter 7.

31. Wayne A. Cornelius, "The Impact of Governmental Performance on Political Attitudes and Behavior," in Francine Rabinowitz and Felicity Trueblood (eds.), *Latin American Urban Research,* Vol. III (Beverly Hills, Calif.: Sage, 1974), tables 3, 4, 5.

32. Wayne A. Cornelius, *Political Learning among the Migrant Poor* (Beverly Hills, Calif.: Sage Professional Papers in Comparative Politics, No. 01-137, 1973).

33. Daniel Goldrich, Raymond B. Pratt, and C. R. Schuller, "The Political Integration of Lower-Class Urban Settlements in Chile and Peru," in Irving Louis Horowitz (ed.), *Masses in Latin America* (New York: Oxford University Press, 1970).

34. Thomas M. Lutz, "Self-Help Neighborhood Organizations, Political Socialization, and the Developing Political Orientations of Urban Squatters in Latin America: Contrasting Patterns from Case Studies in Panama City, Guayaquil, and Lima" (Ph.D. thesis, Georgetown University, 1970); David Collier, "Squatter Settlement Formation and the Politics of Coöptation in Peru" (Ph.D. thesis, University of Chicago, 1971), especially chapters 5 and 6.

35. Kemal H. Karpat, "The Gecekondu: Rural Migration and Urbanization" (Unpublished book manuscript, spring 1972), especially chapter 7, "Politics in the Gecekondu."

36. Donald L. Horowitz, "Race and Politics in Guyana, Trinidad, and Jamaica" (Ph.D. thesis, Harvard University, 1967), table 5.1, p. 138. There is little reason to suspect that either coercion or falsified or inaccurate statistics account for these particular data, according to the author.

37. This summary is based on discussions with Donald L. Horowitz of the Brookings Institution, drawing on his extensive knowledge of patterns of ethnic politics in developing nations.

38. Donald L. Horowitz, "Multiracial Politics in the New States: Toward a Theory of Conflict," in Robert J. Jackson and Michael B. Stein (eds.), *Issues in Comparative Politics* (New York: St. Martin's Press, 1971), pp. 167-72.

39. The concentration of open unemployment among the somewhat better educated and more comfortable job-seekers is documented in David Turnham, *The Employment Problem in Less Developed Countries* (Paris: OECD Development Centre, 1971). Peter Gutkind, discussing urban unemployment in Africa, notes that some job-seekers lower their expectations, "although for Primary School Leavers this is somewhat unusual. Junior Secondary Leavers tend to spend their time scanning the newspapers for advertisements and writing applications . . . " "The Energy of Despair: Social Organization of the Unemployed in Two African Cities: Lagos and Nairobi," *Civilizations,* 17 (1967), p. 34 of the reprint version.

40. In this respect one could contrast the efforts of the Viet Cong and of Che Guevara in Bolivia to organize the rural poor. See Jeffrey Race, *War Comes to Long An* (Berkeley: University of California Press, 1972) for a graphic description of how the Viet Cong demonstrated their power in a rural province.

41. Robert C. Fried, "Urbanization and Italian Politics," *Journal of Politics,* 29 (August 1967), p. 525.

42. For a detailed discussion of the rise of ANAPO and its performance in

1970, see Judith Talbot Campos and John F. McCamant, *Cleavage Shift in Colombia: Analysis of the 1970 Elections* (Beverly Hills, Calif.: Sage Professional Papers, Comparative Politics Series No. 01-032; 1972).

   43. For an excellent summary of the role of the Church in social reform in Latin America, see George C. Lodge, *Engines of Change* (New York: Knopf, 1970), chapter 9, "The Radical Church."

   44. Ray, *Politics of the Barrios,* p. 32, 115ff.

   45. Mathiasen and Powell, "Participation and Efficacy," pp. 319-323 and tables 8 and 10.

6. Conclusion

   1. Zbigniew Brzezinski and Samuel P. Huntington, *Political Power: USA/USSR* (New York: Viking Press, 1964), p. 91.

   2. Samuel P. Huntington, *Political Order in Changing Societies* (New Haven: Yale University Press, 1968), p. 266.

   3. This phenomenon is, of course, the focal point of Mancur Olson's argument in *The Logic of Collective Action* (Cambridge: Harvard University Press, 1965).

   4. The support for this proposition is stated at length in Huntington, *Political Order,* passim.

Index

Index

Publications Written under
the Auspices of the
Center for International Affairs,
Harvard University

Created in 1958, the Center for International Affairs fosters advanced study of basic world problems by scholars from various disciplines and senior officials from many countries. The research at the Center focuses on economic, social, and political development, the management of force in the modern world, the evolving roles of Western Europe and the Communist nations, and the conditions of international order.

BOOKS

The Soviet Bloc, by Zbigniew K. Brzezinski (Sponsored jointly with the Russian Research Center), 1960. Harvard University Press. Revised edition, 1967.

The Necessity for Choice, by Henry A. Kissinger, 1961. Harper & Bros.

Strategy and Arms Control, by Thomas C. Schelling and Morton H. Halperin, 1961. Twentieth Century Fund.

United States Manufacturing Investment in Brazil, by Lincoln Gordon and Engelbert L. Grommers, 1962. Harvard Business School.

The Economy of Cyprus, by A. J. Meyer, with Simos Vassiliou (sponsored jointly with the Center for Middle Eastern Studies), 1962. Harvard University Press.

Communist China 1955-1959: Policy Documents with Analysis, with a foreword by Robert R. Bowie and John K. Fairbank (sponsored jointly with the East Asian Research Center), 1962. Harvard University Press.

Somali Nationalism, by Saadia Touval, 1963. Harvard University Press.

The Dilemma of Mexico's Development, by Raymond Vernon, 1963. Harvard University Press.

Limited War in the Nuclear Age, by Morton H. Halperin, 1963. John Wiley & Sons.

The Arms Debate, by Robert A. Levine, 1963. Harvard University Press.

Africans on the Land, by Montague Yudelman, 1964. Harvard University Press.

Counterinsurgency Warfare, by David Galula, 1964. Frederick A. Praeger, Inc.

People and Policy in the Middle East, by Max Weston Thornburg, 1964. W. W. Norton & Co.

196

Shaping the Future, by Robert R. Bowie, 1964. Columbia University Press.

Foreign Aid and Foreign Policy, by Edward S. Mason (sponsored jointly with the Council on Foreign Relations), 1964. Harper & Row.

How Nations Negotiate, by Fred Charles Iklé, 1964. Harper & Row.

China and the Bomb, by Morton H. Halperin (sponsored jointly with the East Asian Research Center), 1965. Frederick A. Praeger, Inc.

Democracy in Germany, by Fritz Erler (Jodidi Lectures), 1965. Harvard University Press.

The Troubled Partnership, by Henry A. Kissinger (sponsored jointly with the Council on Foreign Relations), 1965. McGraw-Hill Book Co.

The Rise of Nationalism in Central Africa, by Robert I. Rotberg, 1965. Harvard University Press.

Pan-Africanism and East African Integration, by Joseph S. Nye, Jr., 1965. Harvard University Press.

Communist China and Arms Control, by Morton H. Halperin and Dwight H. Perkins (sponsored jointly with the East Asian Research Center), 1965. Frederick A. Praeger, Inc.

Problems of National Strategy, ed. Henry Kissinger, 1965. Frederick A. Praeger, Inc.

Deterrence before Hiroshima: The Airpower Background of Modern Strategy, by George H. Quester, 1966. John Wiley & Sons.

Containing the Arms Race, by Jeremy J. Stone, 1966. M.I.T. Press.

Germany and the Atlantic Alliance: The Interaction of Strategy and Politics, by James L. Richardson, 1966. Harvard University Press.

Arms and Influence, by Thomas C. Schelling, 1966. Yale University Press.

Political Change in a West African State, by Martin Kilson, 1966. Harvard University Press.

Planning without Facts: Lessons in Resource Allocation from Nigeria's Development, by Wolfgang F. Stolper, 1966. Harvard University Press.

Export Instability and Economic Development, by Alasdair I. MacBean, 1966. Harvard University Press.

Foreign Policy and Democratic Politics, by Kenneth N. Waltz (sponsored jointly with the Institute of War and Peace Studies, Columbia University), 1967. Little, Brown & Co.

Contemporary Military Strategy, by Morton H. Halperin, 1967. Little, Brown & Co.

Sino-Soviet Relations and Arms Control, ed. Morton H. Halperin (sponsored jointly with the East Asian Research Center), 1967. M.I.T. Press.

Africa and United States Policy, by Rupert Emerson, 1967. Prentice-Hall.

Elites in Latin America, edited by Seymour M. Lipset and Aldo Solari, 1967. Oxford University Press.

Europe's Postwar Growth, by Charles P. Kindleberger, 1967. Harvard University Press.

The Rise and Decline of the Cold War, by Paul Seabury, 1967. Basic Books.
Student Politics, ed. S. M. Lipset, 1967. Basic Books.
Pakistan's Development: Social Goals and Private Incentives, by Gustav F. Papanek, 1967. Harvard University Press.
Strike a Blow and Die: A Narrative of Race Relations in Colonial Africa, by George Simeon Mwase, ed. Robert I. Rotberg, 1967. Harvard University Press.
Party Systems and Voter Alignments, edited by Seymour M. Lipset and Stein Rokkan, 1967. Free Press.
Agrarian Socialism, by Seymour M. Lipset, revised edition, 1968. Doubleday Anchor.
Aid, Influence, and Foreign Policy, by Joan M. Nelson, 1968. The Macmillan Company.
International Regionalism, by Joseph S. Nye, 1968. Little, Brown & Co.
Revolution and Counterrevolution, by Seymour M. Lipset, 1968. Basic Books.
Political Order in Changing Societies, by Samuel P. Huntington, 1968. Yale University Press.
The TFX *Decision: McNamara and the Military,* by Robert J. Art, 1968. Little, Brown & Co.
Korea: The Politics of the Vortex, by Gregory Henderson, 1968. Harvard University Press.
Political Development in Latin America, by Martin Needler, 1968. Random House.
The Precarious Republic, by Michael Hudson, 1968. Random House.
The Brazilian Capital Goods Industry, 1929-1964 (sponsored jointly with the Center for Studies in Education and Development), by Nathaniel H. Leff, 1968. Harvard University Press.
Economic Policy-Making and Development in Brazil, 1947-1964, by Nathaniel H. Leff, 1968. John Wiley & Sons.
Turmoil and Transition: Higher Education and Student Politics in India, edited by Philip G. Altbach, 1968. Lalvani Publishing House (Bombay).
German Foreign Policy in Transition, by Karl Kaiser, 1968. Oxford University Press.
Protest and Power in Black Africa, edited by Robert I Rotberg, 1969. Oxford University Press.
Peace in Europe, by Karl E. Birnbaum, 1969. Oxford University Press.
The Process of Modernization: An Annotated Bibliography on the Sociocultural Aspects of Development, by John Brode, 1969. Harvard University Press.
Students in Revolt, edited by Seymour M. Lipset and Philip G. Altbach, 1969. Houghton Mifflin.
Agricultural Development in India's Districts: The Intensive Agricultural Districts Programme, by Dorris D. Brown, 1970. Harvard University Press.
Authoritarian Politics in Modern Society: The Dynamics of Established One-

Party Systems, edited by Samuel P. Huntington and Clement H. Moore, 1970. Basic Books.

Nuclear Diplomacy, by George H. Quester, 1970. Dunellen.

The Logic of Images in International Relations, by Robert Jervis, 1970. Princeton University Press.

Europe's Would-Be Polity, by Leon Lindberg and Stuart A. Scheingold, 1970. Prentice-Hall.

Taxation and Development: Lessons from Colombian Experience, by Richard M. Bird, 1970. Harvard University Press.

Lord and Peasant in Peru: A Paradigm of Political and Social Change, by F. LaMond Tullis, 1970. Harvard University Press.

The Kennedy Round in American Trade Policy: The Twilight of the GATT? by John W. Evans, 1971. Harvard University Press.

Korean Development: The Interplay of Politics and Economics, by David C. Cole and Princeton N. Lyman, 1971. Harvard University Press.

Development Policy II—The Pakistan Experience, edited by Walter P. Falcon and Gustav F. Papanek, 1971. Harvard University Press.

Higher Education in a Transitional Society, by Philip G. Altbach, 1971. Sindhu Publications (Bombay).

Studies in Development Planning, edited by Hollis B. Chenery, 1971. Harvard University Press.

Passion and Politics, by Seymour M. Lipset with Gerald Schaflander, 1971. Little, Brown & Co.

Political Mobilization of the Venezuelan Peasant, by John D. Powell, 1971. Harvard University Press.

Higher Education in India, edited by Amrik Singh and Philip Altbach, 1971. Oxford University Press (Delhi).

The Myth of the Guerrilla, by J. Bowyer Bell, 1971. Blond (London) and Knopf (New York).

International Norms and War between States: Three Studies in International Politics, by Kjell Goldmann, 1971. Published jointly by Läromedelsförlagen (Sweden) and the Swedish Institute of International Affairs.

Peace in Parts: Integration and Conflict in Regional Organization, by Joseph S. Nye, Jr., 1971. Little, Brown & Co.

Sovereignty at Bay: The Multinational Spread of U.S. Enterprise, by Raymond Vernon, 1971. Basic Books.

Defense Strategy for the Seventies (revision of *Contemporary Military Strategy*), by Morton H. Halperin, 1971. Little, Brown & Co.

Peasants Against Politics: Rural Organization in Brittany, 1911-1967, by Suzanne Berger, 1972. Harvard University Press.

Transnational Relations and World Politics, edited by Robert O. Keohane and Joseph S. Nye, Jr., 1972. Harvard University Press.

Latin American University Students: A Six Nation Study, by Arthur Liebman,

Kenneth N. Walker, and Myron Glazer, 1972. Harvard University Press.

The Politics of Land Reform in Chile, 1950-1970: Public Policy, Political Institutions, and Social Change, by Robert R. Kaufman, 1972. Harvard University Press.

The Boundary Politics of Independent Africa, by Saadia Touval, 1972. Harvard University Press.

The Politics of Nonviolent Action, by Gene E. Sharp, 1973. Porter Sargent.

System 37 Viggen: Arms, Technology, and the Domestication of Glory, by Ingemar Dörfer, 1973. Universitetsforlaget (Oslo).

University Students and African Politics, by William John Hanna, 1974. Africana Publishing Company.

Organizing the Transnational: The Experience with Transnational Enterprise in Advanced Technology, by M. S. Hochmuth, 1974. Sijthoff (Leiden).

Becoming Modern, by Alex Inkeles and David H. Smith, 1974. Harvard University Press.

Multinational Corporations and the Politics of Dependence: Copper in Chile, by Theodore Moran, 1974. Princeton University Press.

The Andean Group: A Case Study in Economic Integration among Developing Countries, by David Morawetz, 1974. M.I.T. Press.

Kenya: The Politics of Participation and Control, by Henry Bienen, 1974. Princeton University Press.

Land Reform and Politics: A Comparative Analysis, by Hung-chao Tai, 1974. University of California Press.

Big Business and the State: Changing Relations in Western Europe, edited by Raymond Vernon, 1974. Harvard University Press.

Economic Policymaking in a Conflict Society: The Argentine Case, by Richard D. Mallon and Juan V. Sourrouille, 1975. Harvard University Press.

New States in the Modern World, edited by Martin Kilson, 1975. Harvard University Press.

Revolutionary Civil War: The Elements of Victory and Defeat, by David Wilkinson, 1975. Page-Ficklin Publications.

Politics and the Migrant Poor in Mexico City, by Wayne A. Cornelius, 1975. Stanford University Press.

No Easy Choice: Political Participation in Developing Countries, by Samuel P. Huntington and Joan M. Nelson, 1976. Harvard University Press.

The International Politics of Natural Resources, by Zuhayr Mikdashi, 1976. Cornell University Press.

The Oil Crisis, edited by Raymond Vernon, 1976. W. W. Norton & Co.

Harvard Studies in International Affairs*
(*formerly Occasional Papers in International Affairs*)

---

*Available from Harvard University Center for International Affairs, 6 Divinity Avenue, Cambridge, Massachusetts 02138

†Out of print. May be ordered from AMS Press, Inc. 56 East 13th Street, New York, N.Y. 10003

†20. *East and West Pakistan: A Problem in the Political Economy of Regional Planning,* by Md. Anisur Rahman, 1968.

†21. *Internal War and International Systems: Perspectives on Method,* by George A. Kelley and Linda B. Miller, 1969.

†22. *Migrants, Urban Poverty, and Instability in Developing Nations,* by Joan M. Nelson, 1969. 81 pp.

23. *Growth and Development in Pakistan, 1955-1969,* by Joseph J. Stern and Walter P. Falcon, 1970. 94 pp. $3.00.

24. *Higher Education in Developing Countries: A Select Bibliography,* by Philip G. Altbach, 1970. 118 pp. $4.00.

25. *Anatomy of Political Institutionalization: The Case of Israel and Some Comparative Analyses,* by Amos Perlmutter, 1970. 60 pp. $2.50.

†26. *The German Democratic Republic from the Sixties to the Seventies,* by Peter Christian Ludz, 1970. 100 pp.

27. *The Law in Political Integration: The Evolution and Integrative Implications of Regional Legal Processes in the European Community,* by Stuart A. Scheingold, 1971. 63 pp. $2.50.

28. *Psychological Dimensions of U.S.-Japanese Relations,* by Hiroshi Kitamura, 1971. 46 pp. $2.00.

29. *Conflict Regulation in Divided Societies,* by Eric A. Nordlinger, 1972. 137 pp. $4.25.

30. *Israel's Political-Military Doctrine,* by Michael I. Handel, 1973. 101 pp. $3.25.

31. *Italy, NATO, and the European Community: The Interplay of Foreign Policy and Domestic Politics,* by Primo Vannicelli, 1974. 67 + X pp. $3.25.

32. *The Choice of Technology in Developing Countries: Some Cautionary Tales,* by C. Peter Timmer, John Woodward Thomas, Louis T. Wells, Jr., and David Morawetz, 1975. 114 pp. $3.45.

33. *The International Role of the Communist Parties of Italy and France,* by Donald L. M. Blackmer and Annie Kriegel, 1975. 67 + X pp. $2.75.

34. *The Hazards of Peace: A European View of Détente,* by Juan Cassiers, 1976. $6.95, cloth; $2.95, paper.

35. *Oil and the Middle East War: Europe in the Energy Crisis,* by Robert J. Lieber, 1976. $7.45, cloth; $3.45, paper.